Contents

Acknowledgements

The research reported here is the result of three years' observation of a group of children from diverse cultural and linguistic backgrounds attending a Canadian school. I am grateful to the children and their parents for allowing me to be an observer of their play and work. I am also grateful to their teachers for their hospitality and for the efforts they made to amplify my understandings of life in schools.

I was fortunate when beginning graduate school to have the following colleagues, teachers and friends at the University of Alberta, who, although they may not recognise their contributions here, have provided me with words and ideas to appropriate along the way: Marilyn Assheton-Smith, Regna Darnell, Tony Fisher, the late Roseanna Houle, and Carl Urion. Their democratic and respectful teaching provided examples of best practices in welcoming newcomers to an academic community. I am deeply appreciative of their invitation to participation.

The theory underlying this study stresses the social construction of intellectual processes and products, and encourages us to consider that learning is distributed among co-participants in communities of practice. Elaine Day, Linda Hof and Sarah Yip were partners with me in the classroom data collection and each contributed crucially to our understanding of what was happening in these classrooms. Kunwal Arora, Karin Dhaliwal-Rai, Bozena Karwowska, Sarah Yip and Lanny Young collected data in the children's homes and I am grateful for their wise counsel about children and families with complex linguistic resources. I also would like to give special thanks to John Holt, whose editorial assistance amounted to co-participation in the project. At various times, the following read all or part of this manuscript and made many helpful suggestions: June Beynon, Diane Dagenais, Suzanne de Castell, Allyson Julé-Lemke, Yasuko Kanno, Mary Kooy, Thoko Muthwa-Kuehn and Bonny Norton. Surjeet Siddoo provided caring and expert word-processing assistance. Although I did not always take their generous advice (so they cannot be held responsible for the book's shortcomings), I am thankful for the counsel of all those listed.

Financial support for this project was provided by a Simon Fraser University President's Research Grant, a Social Sciences and Humanities Research Council of Canada (SSHRCC) Small Grant, and a SSHRCC Standard Research Grant. I am grateful to these agencies and also to my colleague, Phil Winne, who provided expert advice about grant proposals.

A version of Chapter 4 was published as 'Breaking them up, taking them away: ESL students in grade one', in 1998 in *TESOL Quarterly* 32 (1), 61–84. Parts of the data and analysis presented in Chapters 2 and 3 were published in 'Learning English as a Second Language in kindergarten: A community of practice perspective' in *Canadian Modern Language Review* (University of Toronto Press Inc.) 52 (4), 549–76.

I am grateful to my parents, Jack and Eileen Toohey, and my children, Daniel and Jill Cooper, for their encouragement and inspiration. Daniel and Jill provided insider information on childhood and were patient with a mother who was (as Daniel put it), 'obsessed with writing'. Finally, my husband and friend, Doug Cooper, was a constant and loving support in this, as in so much else. Thank you.

Introduction

> Language and culture are [not] scripts to be acquired as much as they are conversations in which people can participate. The question of who is learning what and how much is essentially a question of what conversations they are part of, and this question is a subset of the more powerful question of what conversations are around to be had in a given culture. (McDermott, 1993: 295)

Second language acquisition (SLA) has often been viewed as the acquisition of cultural and linguistic scripts, and second language research for the last 20 years has been centrally concerned with such questions as who is learning what and how much. McDermott's suggestion that researchers need to situate these questions in investigations of the social relations and cultural practices of groups represents an emerging perspective that challenges the predominant concerns of traditional SLA research.

This book focuses on a common set of circumstances in Canada, the United States, Britain, Australia and New Zealand: increasing numbers of young children from minority language backgrounds are taught in mainstream English medium classrooms. In the early 1990s, several textbooks of teaching methods and approaches for such classrooms appeared (e.g. Faltis, 1993; Genesee, 1994; Gibbons, 1993; Rigg & Allen, 1989). Research accounts of child SLA had been available for some time, primarily framed in terms of children's display over time of particular linguistic features (e.g. Dulay & Burt, 1974; Naiman *et al.*, 1978; Saville-Troike, 1988; Snow, 1987; Snow & Hoefnagel-Höhle, 1978; Swain & Lapkin, 1982; Wong Fillmore, 1979; and many others). As Ellis (1998) reminds us, teachers' and researchers' concerns often differ greatly, and the methodological writers tended to focus on techniques and activities teachers might use to enhance learning, while much of the research assessed linguistically-defined aspects of students' learning. Neither the methodological nor the research literature reflected

1

the work of several scholars in a variety of fields that criticised previous conceptualisations of language, learning and learners.

I refer to the work of researchers and theorists in linguistics, sociology, psychology, education, anthropology and philosophy that stressed the importance of the social, cultural, political and economic contexts and practices of language and learners (e.g. Bourdieu, 1977, 1984; Cole, 1992; Foucault, 1972, 1979; Gumperz, 1992; Kress, 1989, 1991, 1993; Lave, 1988; Levine, 1990; Rogoff, 1990; Taylor, 1989). Vygotsky's work describing the sociality of learning, and Bakhtin's notion that speakers struggled to 'appropriate voices' in particular cultural and historical activities and contexts, were increasingly discussed in educational literature (e.g. Appel & Lantolf, 1994; Hall, 1993; Moll, 1994; Wells & Chang-Wells, 1992). Second language educators, particularly those working with adult learners, were urging consideration of second language learning as situated social practice (e.g. Kramsch, 1993; Norton Peirce, 1989; Pennycook, 1990). These poststructural, sociocultural and critical perspectives challenged traditional ways of understanding SLA.

In 1993, I began to teach a course to practising and prospective classroom teachers who found increasing numbers of learners from minority language backgrounds in their classrooms. The textbooks mentioned above, discussing pedagogical approaches for mainstreaming minority language background children, helped me work with participants in my courses, as did some of the research literature. However, I also wanted to talk with my students about how to understand the SLA of children in terms of recently developed poststructural, sociocultural and critical perspectives. Not much classroom research of this latter sort was then available, especially concerning young children. I began this research as a way to fill this gap.

Most of my students were teaching or preparing to teach in primary and/or elementary classrooms. I decided to observe, therefore, in primary classrooms, and I was able to form relationships in an elementary school that enabled me to follow initially six, and finally four, children of minority language backgrounds through three years in their kindergarten, Grade 1 and Grade 2 classrooms. Although designated by their school as 'English as a Second Language (ESL) students', I have both resisted this designation and tried to make it problematic throughout this book, preferring the circumlocution 'children of minority language backgrounds', however cumbersome. I discuss this issue further in Chapters 3 and 4.

Foundational to this research was the notion that investigating the specific circumstances and contexts of learning would be important in helping me understand the range of ways in which languages might be learned and used. Recognising that children who are learning a majority language in a majority language milieu learn in many different contexts besides classrooms, I nevertheless wished to focus on classroom activities and practices to investigate how these create possibilities for engagement in particular kinds of conversations. In this sense I wanted to examine the classroom as a kind of bounded community, with specific practices. Educators probably have more extensive and immediate possibilities for observation and intervention in classroom practices than they might in familial, neighbourhood, ethnic group and larger social and cultural contexts. Examining carefully the practices in the contexts in which we have some influence seemed urgently important to me in helping teachers to find effective ways of responding to these learners.

THIS STUDY

In Chapter 1, I briefly survey some examples of child SLA research from the 1970s and 1980s, and their conceptions of learners and the processes of SLA. I then survey the work of several poststructural, sociocultural and critical theorists, emphasising implications for studying both identity formation and language learning at school. I then introduce my basic research questions, the setting of the research and the methodology.

In Chapter 2, I describe the kindergarten classroom and introduce each of the six focal children, describing events over the course of that kindergarten year. I also present information gathered in teacher and parent interviews about each child. I use these descriptions to analyze how school practices constructed 'school identities' for the children.

Chapter 3 discusses the practices of school with respect to assigning identities to children. I show how each child came to have a school identity that was consequential and also seemed relatively fixed and unitary. As well as finding out what kinds of identities seemed available to each child, I consider what the range of identities reveals about the classroom as a community.

In Chapter 4, I examine physical, material and intellectual practices in the Grade 1 classroom, arguing that participation in these practices shaped access to classroom resources, including the vital resource of conversations with peers and with the teacher. I analyze the variable distribution of these resources in classrooms as economic practices, and argue that these, like school identity practices, are neither natural nor inevitable, but that they have profound effects on learning.

Chapter 5 follows the children to Grade 2; in this chapter, I examine discourse practices that, I argue, regulated children's access to possibilities for appropriation of powerful and desirable voices in their community. I examine how discourse practices in children's Language Arts lessons were organised, and extend the earlier analysis of how classroom practices establish social relations that determine access to classroom resources and ultimately to learning.

In Chapter 6, I discuss theoretical, methodological, and pedagogical ideas and problems emerging through the course of the research, in order to outline possible future approaches to investigating the SLA of young children. I also examine issues raised by this work with regard to longitudinal ethnographic research. Finally, I discuss how schools and teachers might support children of minority language backgrounds in their struggle to appropriate English in public school classrooms.

CHAPTER 1

Framing Story: Theory, Setting and Methodology

When language is systematically unavailable to some, it is important that we not limit our explanations to the traits of the persons involved; it is equally essential that we take into account the interactional circumstances that position the people in the world with a differential access to the common tongue. (McDermott, 1993: 283)

Educational researchers have commonly used the traits of learners to explain schooling outcomes and second language acquisition (SLA) research has often taken learners' characteristics as a central concern. McDermott argues that such a view is limited and that observers need to pay attention to the positions of speakers and their social relations (their 'interactional circumstances'). This chapter surveys how SLA research has addressed these matters in the past and how it might in the future address them.

Larsen-Freeman (1991) argued that SLA research over the past 20 years had had two main preoccupations: the cognitive processes of language acquisition and the effects of learners' characteristics on these processes. Because this research is so well known and because I wish to outline here an alternative approach to investigating second language learning, I will only briefly review previous child SLA research, focusing on a few representative studies, and summarising how SLA research has typically conceptualised learners and the process of language learning. I intend in this chapter to outline how an emphasis on the pivotal role of social interaction both with respect to identity and with respect to learning offers new perspectives for investigating young children's second language learning. I review, therefore, the work of several sociocultural, poststructural and critical theorists to explore how research might investigate second language learning research from such perspectives, discussing how I used these alternatives to develop the theoretical framework and methodology for this study.

LEARNERS AND LEARNING IN SECOND LANGUAGE ACQUISITION RESEARCH

The study of SLA developed rapidly in the 1970s and 1980s as a result of many disciplines' interest in learners' cognitive processes. Inspired by the new science of psycholinguistics, SLA research was influenced by Chomskian notions of language as a rule-governed system, of learning as an individual psychological cognitive process, and of learners as active agents formulating rules for their language outputs. From its inception, SLA research has commonly conceptualised individuals as attached to their individual characteristics. Taylor (1989, 1994) traced the origin of this idea of individuals having specific attributes, abilities and motivations to Western European thought and practices in the 17th and 18th centuries. The assumption of individuals having unique, fixed and coherent 'essences' in congruence with which they learn, think and act has been, Taylor argued, authoritative in Western religious, economic, political, familial, and artistic practices and has persisted into the 20th century. These essences are variously described as souls, personalities, characters, preferences, tendencies and so on; individuals' social locations have been seen as relatively superficial aspects of their personhood, not necessarily even affecting 'core' characteristics. Sampson (1989: 919) noted that from this perspective: 'Individuals are assumed to have personal ownership of the identities they possess, including all of their attributes ... as well as the outcomes of whatever achievements their particular abilities and motivations bring to them.' McNamee (1992) observed that most psychological researchers who have accepted this notion of individual identities are concerned with finding (through careful and controlled observation) the basic structure or essence of individual identities.

The study of learners' characteristics (age, intelligence, aptitude, motivation, learning styles, and so on) and their effects on internalisation of linguistic 'input', was, as Larsen-Freeman observed, the subject of several studies. An early and influential SLA study entitled *The Good Language Learner* (Naiman *et al.*, 1978), building on earlier ideas of Rubin (1975), examined both the cognitive processes of language acquisition and the effects of learner characteristics on these processes. Naiman *et al.* (1978: 3) were interested in language learners' mental strategies ('perceiving, analyzing, classifying, relating, storing, receiving and constructing a language output'), as well as the relationships between the personalities, learning styles, motivations and other (what they considered) individually owned characteristics of individual learners and their acquisition of second languages. The authors hypothesised that good language learners (both adults and children) have different mental strategies and traits from poor language learners. They drew their evidence of language learning from self-reports by adults and from performance on a series of proficiency tests by children. Although the study revealed little empirical support for the hypothesis of differential strategic processing of second language input, and only weak support for the notion that good language learners had distinctive traits or characteristics, the authors argued that better methods for demonstrating internal processing and for assessing personality and cognitive characteristics would strengthen support for the hypothesis.

In addition to consideration of what individual learners bring to second language learning, traditional SLA research has investigated processes assumed to go on in these atomistic learners' brains as they internalise second language knowledge. Dulay *et al.* (1982: 276) described the cognitive processes of language acquisition as those 'by which language learners gradually organise the language they hear, according to the rules they construct to understand and generate sentences'. Davis (1995: 428) argued that this psychological or 'mentalist' model was 'designed to get at language learners' mental strategies in acquiring an L2'. A great deal of research on both child and adult SLA used data from learner productions and self-reflections to induce generalisations about learners' 'subconscious' processes of organisation, rule construction and sentence generation (Dulay & Burt, 1974; Hakuta, 1974; Huang & Hatch, 1978). Through a focus initially on the systematicity of learner errors (Corder, 1967; Ravem, 1968; Richards, 1974; Selinker, 1972) and later of learner productions as a whole (Hatch, 1978; Schachter, 1988; Schachter & Celce-Murcia, 1977), researchers investigated processes by which adults and children internalised linguistic rules. With the discovery of a regular order in acquisition of English grammatical morphemes, researchers hypothesised a universal process of language acquisition. Research on learner productions and the plotting of emergent grammars led to attempts to understand both how internalisation of linguistic knowledge occurred and how knowledge of these processes might be of practical, pedagogical benefit (Ellis, 1994; Larsen-Freeman & Long, 1991).

In a study of child second language learners, Wong Fillmore (1979: 221) looked for the 'combination of interests, inclinations, skills, temperament, needs and motivations' that distinguished good from poor second language learners. She concluded that individual motivation to identify with people who speak English was responsible for the differential rates of acquisition by the children in her study. Strong (1983: 255), in a later study of kindergarten children learning ESL, found support for 'a relationship between aspects of sociability or outgoingness and natural communicative language skills'.[1] Saville-Troike (1988) investigated relations between child ESL learners' level of cognitive development, their social orientation and learning style and the quantity and quality of their private speech. All this work saw cognitive development, social orientation and learning style as internal aspects of the individuals who 'own' them. However, none of this research considered how social relations among learners, as well as among learners and those who judge their performances, might affect judgements of cognition, social adjustment or learning styles.

LEARNERS AS SOCIALLY/HISTORICALLY/POLITICALLY CONSTRUCTED

Recently, theorists from a variety of disciplines have mounted critiques of the conceptualisation of both individuals and groups as learning, thinking and acting in accord with essences independent of the social relations within which they act. Some feminist theory, for example, has criticised hypotheses about essential distinctions between women and men for denying the multiplicity of experiences and aspirations of humans and for promoting 'repressively stereotypic norms of gender appropriateness' (Bryson & de Castell, 1997: 98). Gal (1991: 176) argued that rather than a set of stable characteristics or essences, gender is 'a system of culturally constructed relations of power, produced and reproduced in interaction between and among men and women'. For Gal, conceptualisations of women and men as members of groups with stable or essential characteristics did not do justice to how local, unstable power relations shape experience.

Cultural theorists also critiqued the practice of ascribing more or less stable constellations of characteristics, both 'positive' and 'negative' to groups and individuals defined on the basis of culture. Hall (1990: 225), for example, argued for a notion of cultural identity as situated in 'time, history and culture':

> Cultural identity is not a fixed essence at all, lying unchanged outside history and culture. It is not some universal and transcendental spirit inside us on which history has made no fundamental mark . . . . Not an essence but a positioning. (Hall, 1990: 226)

Gal's and Hall's arguments about gender and cultural identity represent much contemporary work on identity in general. Seeing identity not as an essence, but as a positioning, helps us to focus on the social construction of that positioning, the politics of position. From this perspective, identity is unstable, constructed in particular local interactions and entails relationships of power.

Poststructural theorist Foucault directed much of his work toward understanding how positioning practices operate in contemporary Western cultures. He described these processes as occurring through people's discourse, which 'systematically forms the objects about which they speak' (Foucault, 1972: 49), providing metrics and hierarchies for categorising people. Hierarchies provide norms and enable the articulation of standards so that people can be compared and differentiated on the basis of their relation to standards. Foucault contended that the judgements made by others with regard to these norms are judgements that impose a 'law of truth' on individuals:

> This form of power applies itself to immediate everyday life which categorises the individual, marks him by his own individuality, attaches him to his own identity, imposes a law of truth on him which he must recognise and which others have to recognise in him. (Foucault, 1972: 212)

Foucault observed that the practices of categorising individuals and attaching them to their identities were enacted in particular institutions (like prisons and schools) in Western Europe, beginning in the 17th and 18th centuries. Individuals, then, were constructed by the practices of the institutions with which they were engaged. He further argued that individuals categorised as too far from a norm undergo sanctions to 'normalise' them (Foucault, 1979).

Some authors have been critical of the ways in which SLA research has conceptualised learners as having no particular social locations or histories, and a collection of papers by various authors in a recent special topic issue of *TESOL Quarterly* (Norton, 1997a) applied some current feminist, cultural and poststructural theories about identity to the study of second language learning. For these authors, much SLA research has characterised learners in simplistic ways that do not take dynamism over time and place into account. Similarly, these authors see SLA research as unable to account satisfactorily for power relations in learning events.

LEARNING AS SOCIALLY/HISTORICALLY/POLITICALLY CONSTRUCTED

Not only conceptualisations about language learners but also conceptualisations about the processes of language learning have been recently subject to criticism from a number of directions. Davis (1995), for example, has criticised the assumption in SLA research that language learning is solely a mental process, occurring within the brains of individual learners; she called for socially situated SLA studies, which would see language learning as a process embedded in its sociocultural contexts. Snow (1992, 1993) pointed out that while psycholinguistically oriented SLA research has effectively delineated the complexity both of second language learning and of second language learners, it has been less successful in recognising the social and cultural situatedness of language learning and use.

Some second language learning studies that take this socially situated view are increasingly becoming available (e.g. Appel & Lantolf, 1994; Bourne, 1992; Gutierrez & Larson, 1994; Kanno & Applebaum, 1995; Norton, 2000; Vasquez *et al.*, 1994; Willett, 1995). I review their specific contributions to my study in various places later. These researchers have been informed by work in a variety of disciplines. Some have consulted scholarship in psychology that investigated aspects of the sociocultural contexts in which children and adults learn and function (e.g. Cole, 1996, 1998; Rogoff *et al.*, 1996; Wertsch, 1991, 1998). The contributions of linguists, sociolinguists and anthropologists have also provided important background (e.g. Duranti & Goodwin, 1992; Goodwin, 1990; Ochs, 1988). All these scholars have seen the work of Lev S. Vygotsky, Mikhail M. Bakhtin, and their contemporaries, as foundational to the development of what is variously termed a sociocultural, socio-historical or cultural-historical perspective. In the next section, I review aspects of Vygotsky's and Bakhtin's work that have provided background to the current study. Many of these Soviet scholars' ideas are reflected in the work of

American anthropologists Jean Lave and Etienne Wenger, who provide ways to investigate how the social practices of sociocultural contexts are constitutive of the learning that occurs in them. Taken together, the work of these theorists provide new ways to examine the social practices of second language learning and teaching.

THE SOCIALITY OF DEVELOPMENT

Many writers have recognised the ideas of the Russian psychologist Vygotsky and his colleagues as important in the study of language acquisition (e.g. Cazden, 1993; Goodman & Goodman, 1994; Johnson, 1995; Moll, 1994; Packer, 1993; Trueba *et al.*, 1981; Wells & Chang-Wells, 1992) and their ideas provide important foundational theory for the present study. Vygotsky's emphasis on the social construction of learning (with regard not only to participants in instructional events, but also with regard to what 'counts as' necessary or desirable learning), permits researchers to examine classroom events and practices, and the ways in which particular children participate in these, as situated in larger, concentric circles of context (Vygotsky, 1978, 1986).

Recognising that psychologists had traditionally examined individual develop-ment and functioning, Vygotsky and his colleagues in the post-revolutionary Soviet Union aimed to establish a psychology congruent with Marxist ideas about the importance of social relations in human development and functioning (cf. Measures *et al.*, 1997; Rosa & Montero, 1994). For these Soviet theorists, the social world is constitutive of humans (as well as constituted by humans), not just a surrounding context for them. This basic idea of the reflexivity of individuals and their social worlds makes Vygotsky's work different from much Western psychology, which has tended to see individual development as independent of social relations (Wertsch, 1991).

Vygotsky's observation that children's mental processes are constructed through relationships with others (often adults) provides a basis for his interest in the social formation of individuals. He observed and called attention to mental processes in children evident in relationships with others (as in joint problem-solving with more skilled partners) that were not evident when the children were alone. He theorised the phenomenon of a child functioning 'as though he were a head taller than himself' in social interaction as a child's potential area of growth, a child's 'zone of proximal development' (Vygotsky, 1978: 102). As Rogoff *et al.* (1993: 232) put it, more skilled partners 'bring the intellectual tools of society within the reach of children' and thus facilitate activity leading to growth.

Vygotsky used the notion of the zone of proximal development to focus attention on the sociality of learning and on children's potentials and future growth. Educa-tional literature increasingly invokes the notion of the zone of proximal development as a theoretical support for recommended instructional practices, espe-cially the provision of supportive 'scaffolding' for students (through collaboration with peers, for example). Seeing this matter somewhat differently, Rogoff *et al.*

observed that although many researchers focus on interpersonal relationships between children and more skilled partners:

> Such analysis is incomplete unless it also considers the societal basis of the shared problem-solving – the nature of the problem the partners seek to solve, the values involved in determining the appropriate goals and means, the intellectual tools available (e.g. the language and number systems, literacy, and mnemonic devices), and the institutional structures of the interaction (e.g. schooling and political and economic systems). (Rogoff *et al.*, 1993: 232)

As these authors pointed out, the social world presents itself universally, not only in the fact that more than one person is usually involved in observable instructional events. The books, the problems, what gets defined as 'skilled performance', the intellectual tools (e.g. language choices) and the situation itself are as permeated with sociality as are the interactants. This perspective enjoins observers to examine the social construction of learning not only with respect to the interactants but also with respect to the social milieu in which those interactants are situated, with respect to the tools they use, the problems with which they engage, and so on. Such an approach allows the observer to conceptualise learning events as occurring in wider and wider circles of context.

From this perspective, things could always be otherwise: what an adult chooses to teach a child in a particular situation, or what a school system deems important to learn, or what a nation decides must be taught its citizens, or what a textbook writer considers essential aspects of a second language, have no necessary or 'natural' inevitability, if they are all socially constructed. Classrooms, for example, appear as 'artificial creations . . . organised around beliefs and practices that control and regulate the intellectual life of students' (Moll, 1992: 23).

This wider cultural and historical focus on sociality does not figure much in second language instructional literature; rather, such literature rather abstractly stresses the social conditions and origins of learning, but thereafter commonly focuses on assessing and describing individual internalisation of the second language. Sociality is dismissed, so to speak, as a background to individual internalisation. Many theorists have criticised the very notion of internalisation (cf. Packer, 1993), arguing that it inadequately represents how learners gain from social interaction. Rogoff *et al.* (1993: 234) suggested that the process might be better thought of as appropriation, so as to emphasise that learners, already participants in activities, learn to manage them, rather than 'engaging in a two stage process of first, social lessons, and then individual internalisation to put these lessons inside their heads'. This perspective would see second language learning, then, as a process of appropriating the second language in specific situations and learning to manage the activities (the conversations, perhaps, in McDermott's, 1993, terms) of a particular context.

If second language learning is a process of appropriation, what do learners appropriate? Wertsch *et al.* (1995: 11) stated that the 'goal of a sociocultural approach is to explicate the relationships between human action, on the one hand, and the cultural, institutional, and historical situations in which this action occurs, on the other', and they further argued that 'mediations' provide the link between actions and situations. Vygotsky (1981) saw language as a socially constructed intellectual tool, a 'mediation' used in action. Also in Vygotsky's (1978) view, human beings mediate their interactions with one another through the use of culturally and historically formed artifacts; for him, participation in social activities is importantly mediated by the use of language.[2] Mediations can be studied in terms of how they have achieved their particular formulation socially, historically and politically in the concrete circumstances of their use (cf. Wertsch, 1998, for an illustration of this approach).

One important contribution of Vygotsky's thought is the notion that material mediations or tools in many ways parallel 'psychological tools': natural languages, counting systems, mnemonic devices, writing, signs, and so on (Wertsch, 1991). Seeing language as a tool, parallel in some ways to a material tool, radically departs from psychology's habit of seeing language as part of (or at least, housed in) the mind. From a Vygotskian perspective, a second language could be seen as one among many mediating means people use to participate in social activities. Investigation of second language learning, then, would include investigation of how variously located newcomers use these mediational means in their particular contexts. How social activities are organised in any particular location will affect how newcomers come to appropriate the use of these tools.

THE DIALOGIC PERSPECTIVE

Mikhail M. Bakhtin's work on aspects of human speech suggests ways to think about language as a mediating means. Like Vygotsky, Bakhtin (1981) believed in the importance of studying action situated in specific sociocultural contexts. With regard to context, he argued that understanding social events required attention not only to speakers' and listeners' contemporary and historical social positioning, but also to past, present and future linguistic contexts. For him, language is situated in a 'chain of speech communication' of past, present and future utterances and discourses on the same and related topics. Bakhtin understood that speakers construct their messages in response to previous messages (from differently situated speakers) and in anticipation of future responses (again, by different 'voices'). Thus, utterances are 'dialogically' linked to one another. Bakhtin's work on dialogism is informative with respect to the investigation of the appropriation of classroom language.

Wertsch (1991) considered dialogicality – voices coming into contact – the most basic theoretical construct in Bakhtin's work. Dialogicality refers to participation in the 'communicative chain': the exchange of utterances structured by the tension between the voices of speakers and of their listeners (and previous and future speakers and listeners) (cf. Nystrand *et al.*, 1997). Language events are thus joint productions: speakers construct their utterances on the basis of their interaction with listeners, both in actual and assumed communities. The interlocutors' social positions matter, as do previous and future speakers' and hearers' positions; hence, 'finding a place' in the chain of speech communication is difficult and complex.

Bakhtin returned in different ways to this struggle to come to voice. He spoke of the struggle for ownership of language, the need for speakers to wrest language from other people's mouths and intentions:

> Words are, initially, the other's words, and at foremost, the mother's words. Gradually, these 'alien words' change, dialogically, to become one's 'own alien words' until they are transformed into 'one's own words'. (Bakhtin, 1984: 385, cited in Smolka *et al.*, 1995: 18, their translation of Bakhtin)

> The word in language is half someone else's. It becomes 'one's own' only when the speaker populates it with his own intention, his own accent, when he appropriates the word, adapting it to his own semantic and expressive intention. Prior to this moment of appropriation, the word does not exist in a neutral and impersonal language (it is not, after all, out of a dictionary that a speaker gets his words!) but rather it exists in other people's mouths, in other people's concrete contexts, serving other people's intentions: it is from there that one must take the word and make it one's own. (Bakhtin, 1981: 293–4)

For Bakhtin, individuals never solely create utterances, either out of their own 'individualised' psychological reality, or through application of the rules of a syntactic system. Speakers try on other people's utterances; they take words from other people's mouths; they appropriate these utterances and gradually (but not without conflict) these utterances come to serve their needs and relay their meanings.

> We come to know our native language – its lexical composition and grammatical structure – not from dictionaries and grammars but from concrete utterances which we hear and which we ourselves reproduce in live speech communication with people around us. We assimilate forms of language only in forms of utterances . . . [They] enter our experience and consciousness together. (Bakhtin, 1986: 78)

Like Vygotsky, then, Bakhtin stressed the sociality of intellectual products as well as of intellectual processes. Persons can use their 'voices', when they can enter the communicative chain, as they initially appropriate others' utterances and bend these utterances to their own intentions. Dialogicality for Bakhtin is how speakers get past ventriloquation (using other people's language) in order to enter the communicative chain, for in finding words to answer another speaker's utterance, a person finds and expresses voice.

Bakhtin's observations about the sociality of speech and language and the development of voice and dialogicality can enormously influence how research approaches second language learning. Rather than seeing second language learners as gradually internalising and applying the rules of a variety of systems (syntactic, phonological, semantic, pragmatic and so on) of a standard language, Bakhtin's work encourages our perceiving beginners in a language as doing the complicated linguistic, social and psychological work of constructing 'voices' within a specific community and at the same time, constructing a point of view, a 'speaking subject's perspective, conceptual horizon, intention and world view' (Wertsch, 1991: 51).

If learners struggle to appropriate others' voices and to 'bend' these to their own purposes, if learners' and their interlocutors' past, present and future social positioning crucially affect how they manage that appropriation, and if by participating in language or coming to voice learners find answering words for others' words, attention to those others and to the learners' social contexts is critically important. Anthropologists Jean Lave and Etienne Wenger (1991) provided examples of how learning in a variety of contexts is centrally a matter of social practice.

COMMUNITIES OF PRACTICE

Although Vygotsky's work attended to context in terms of macro-societal practices and groupings as well as (usually) dyads engaged in explicitly instructional processes, Lave and Wenger were concerned with what they called 'communities of practice': relations between groups of people engaged in specific, local, historically constructed, changing practices, of which only some might be intentionally instructional. For them:

> A community of practice is a set of relations among persons, activity, and world, over time and in relation with other tangential and overlapping communities of practice. (Lave & Wenger, 1991: 98)

Membership in these communities shifts and newcomers participate (in 'attenuated ways') with old-timers in the performance of community practices. Lave and Wenger suggested the notion of 'legitimate peripheral participation' to describe the engagement in community practices of all participants who have varied degrees of familiarity with the practices of the community.

Lave and Wenger offered ways to move away from individualistic notions of learning. Summarising their view, Hanks observed:

> Learning is a process that takes place in a participation framework, not in an individual mind . . . It is the community, or at least those participating in the learning context, who 'learn' under this definition. Learning is, as it were, distributed among coparticipants, not a one-person act. (Hanks, 1991: 15)

> Rather than asking what kinds of cognitive processes and conceptual structures are involved, they ask what kind of social engagements provide the proper context for learning to take place. (Hanks, 1991: 14)

Lave and Wenger's (1991) volume is one among an increasing number of publications in which psychologists, anthropologists, philosophers and educators propose what they variously term situated cognition, sociocultural, socio-historical or cultural-historical theory, all of which 'seek to better reflect the fundamentally social nature of learning and cognition' (Kirshner & Whitson, 1997: 1). For these theorists, moving focus from the individual to settings and activities has permitted analysis of relations within settings (defined more or less broadly) and examination of the learning that inevitably accompanies social practice. Communities may provide more or less desirable, powerful or equitable positions for participants within them, but – through the practices in which participants engage – all participants learn. What they might learn is shaped by the kinds of positions they might occupy. Some might even learn something like 'assume a minimal role in this activity'. Lave & Wenger (1991: 98) noted that the 'social structure of the community of practice, its power relations and its conditions for legitimacy define possibilities for learning (i.e. for legitimate peripheral participation)'.

This perspective, which emphasises the importance of the social in human action, has been recognised by some as only a partial solution to developing a comprehensive view of cognition. Collins (1993) has argued that the social theory underlying some sociocultural work leans toward a social determinism, which Kirshner and Whitson (1997: 7) argued, 'undervalues the productive possibilities of everyday conflicts and contradictions'. Forman *et al.* (1993: 6) pointed out that an emphasis on the sociocultural contexts of human beings should not obscure from view 'real people who develop a variety of interpersonal relationships with one another in the course of their shared activity in a given institutional context'. These authors all share a concern that understandings of learning and action take seriously into account both social practices, but also individual performance and understandings of those practices. I discuss these matters in more detail in Chapters 3 and 6.

In the classrooms in which I observed, I examined participants (including myself) as members of overlapping communities of practice. I saw each classroom as a community of practice, as a set of relations among a group of people who engaged together in common practices or activities. However, there were, as well, overlapping communities in those classrooms (e.g. children who spoke Polish at school, children who played soccer at recess, teachers who belonged to specialist associations and so on). It was helpful in my work to see the classroom as the primary community of interest so as to focus on its social structure, including the positions it provided for learners, as well as on the design and structure of the practices that bound it.

RESEARCH QUESTIONS

I have been interested in how children's second language learning might be approached from a perspective which conceptualises learners and learning processes differently from previous approaches. Overall, my aim has been to find ways to take learners' 'interactional circumstances' into account in constructing descriptions and explanations of how they learn second languages.

Much SLA research, coming as it has from a psychological background, has focused on how individuals, seen as collections of more or less invariant cognitive traits, affective orientations, past experiences and other individual characteristics, engage in the mental processes of second language learning. The latter consists of 'perceiving, analyzing, classifying, relating, storing, retrieving, and constructing a language output' (Naiman *et al.*, 1978: 3): an individual cognitive phenomenon of internalisation of second language knowledge. Some SLA researchers have referred to aspects of the social (in addition to the psychological or cognitive) context, or the environment of second language learning, but as Davis (1995) pointed out, this work commonly sees context solely as a 'modifier' of an individual language learner's internal activity.

My research takes a different perspective both on learners and learning. I reviewed feminist, cultural and poststructural theorists' positions on identity as socially constructed, contradictory, dynamic, and entailing power. I considered Foucault's notion that the practices of institutions with which they are affiliated or by which they are regulated, construct ranked individuals. I have also tried to apply Vygotsky's and Bakhtin's ideas, as well as those of other contemporary advocates of similar sociocultural, socio-historical or cultural-historical theories who have argued that relations and practices among members of communities constitute those members' learning. From this perspective, the researcher sees learners' identities, as well as their learning constructed in the practices of the communities in which they are situated. The theory also recognises that some participants have more access to and more experience in the use of various of the community's mediating means (e.g. language) than others, and that some participants are more and some less advantageously positioned in their community. A classroom being a kind of community, one can examine its practices not only in terms of how they identify learners and how the learners take up and are assigned identities, but also in terms of how differential access to the classroom language arises. For children learning a second language, part of constructing voices for themselves is coming to be seen as particular sorts of 'selves' in their school community, that is, coming to have identities as school children. I wish here to investigate how the children of minority language background in my study came to inhabit (temporarily and in contradictory ways) particular identities in their classrooms. I have also tried to understand how those identities might determine or affect what these children can do and say and in what kinds of conversations they are permitted to engage. Thus, the questions which I apply to this research include this general question:

(1)   What are some of the ways in which the focal children engage with each other and their teacher over the course of their primary schooling?

and these more specific questions:

(2)   How do identity practices affect the access of the focal minority language background children to classroom conversations and thus to possibilities for appropriating voice?
(3)   How do physical, material and intellectual resource distribution practices affect the access of the focal minority language background children to classroom conversations and thus to possibilities for appropriating voice?
(4)   How do discourse practices affect the access of the focal minority language background children to classroom conversations and thus to possibilities for appropriating voice?

These latter questions revolve around aspects of classroom practice and I address each separately in the three successive classrooms – the kindergarten, the Grade 1 classroom and the Grade 2 classroom respectively. Before proceeding to these questions, however, I close this chapter with a description of the site of the research and the methodology I employed.

THE RESEARCH SITE

The suburban city in which Suburban School[3] sits has a population of about 300,000, an area of about 400 square kilometres and great diversity in its residents' socio-economic circumstances and micro-geographic environments. Although it has had a reputation as being physically unattractive, tough and crime-ridden, and its citizens are sometimes locally depicted as uneducated and lower class, in fact, the suburb contains many middle class neighbourhoods, as well as wealthy neighbourhoods of large expensive houses on sizeable acreage. In other parts of the suburb, the urban sprawl which gives the city its reputation is evident, with wide, busy streets lined with strip malls and large areas of low-rental housing. About 25% of the population of Suburban City as a whole speak languages other than or in addition to English and they have greatly diverse linguistic and cultural backgrounds. The Punjabi Sikhs are the only ethnic group to have a 'quarter' (although many other Sikhs live throughout the city), with a temple, homes, retail stores, restaurants and other service and commercial centres clustered within a roughly six-block radius. Members of the other ethnic-linguistic groups live individually and in small clusters all over the city.

Suburban School sits in an area of the city regarded as among the less attractive, adjacent to a busy four-lane arterial access for a major highway. A large shopping mall is located about a kilometer away from the school. Adjacent to the school's playgrounds are a rent-controlled townhouse complex, a secondary school's playing fields and streets of small, mostly well-kept lower-middle and working-class single-family residences. The 1996 census information on family income and education levels places this neighbourhood as working class. Census information lists English, Punjabi, Chinese, Polish, Vietnamese and Tagalog as languages spoken by residents in the school catchment area. People consider the area around the school fairly dangerous at night because of several incidents of youth and sexual violence in the last few years; like many parents, parents of children in the school are generally concerned about child safety issues.

Parental concerns about the safety of minority children might have increased by the beating murder of an elderly Sikh man not far from Suburban School during the time of my research. The accused killers had links to a white suprema- cist group. Safety concerns might also have been increased by a newspaper report that an organiser from the Aryan Resistance Movement, another white supremacist organisation, claimed to have student members in Suburban City schools.

Suburban School, an elementary public school (kindergarten to Grade 7) where this research was conducted, was built more than 40 years ago and is visibly run down. Enrolment over the three years of the research was almost 400 children, but decreased somewhat over the course of those years: the principal believed that some catchment area parents became concerned about the building's age and enrolled their children elsewhere. Many classrooms are uncomfortably hot in the summer and all are dusty. Much of the equipment is old and worn, although there is a new computer laboratory with new, expensive computers. As many as seven classes are held in portables. The gymnasium is in a building unconnected to the school and the children have to go outside to reach it. Heating in the buildings is unpredictable. Specialists like the Learning Assistance teachers, ESL teachers and counsellors have small instructional areas carved out of classrooms. The school district has several schools in such poor condition; it has struggled in times of reduced govern- ment funds and generally growing enrolments to respond adequately to needs for repair and renewal of schools.

Many of the approximately 30 teachers at Suburban School have been there for several years. They express the opinion that this is a good school in which to work and that the children and their parents appreciate their efforts. When interviewed for teaching positions at Suburban School, all were asked about their willingness to work with children who speak English as a second language. School district records indicate that almost 50% of the children at the school come from homes where languages other than English are spoken.

METHODOLOGY

I used ethnographic research methodology in this study resulting in a three-year longitudinal project. Fieldwork began in October 1994. After gaining approval from all agencies concerned, I met first with the principal, and later, the kindergarten teacher, Mrs Clark, and finally, with her class. Consent forms, sent home with the children, were returned, indicating parents' permission for me to observe their children.

Among the 19 children in this kindergarten in 1994, Mrs Clark identified 11 as native speakers of English and eight as English as second language (ESL) learners. These minority language background children came from homes where Laotian, Punjabi, Polish and Chinese were used. I finally selected the six focal children after about three visits. I selected the two children in the class (a boy and a girl) whose home language was Punjabi; the two children in the class (a boy and a girl) whose home language was Polish and 2 (a boy and a girl) of the three children in the class whose home language was Chinese. Which Chinese language(s) these children spoke was not obvious from their registration information, Mrs Clark was not sure and the children did not respond to questions about this.[4] I selected the children I did partly because a boy and a girl from each of these language backgrounds were enrolled (eliminating the single boy who spoke Laotian in the class), and partly because Mrs Clark advised that the third Chinese-speaking child was a very experienced English speaker, and indistinguishable in proficiency from the children whose families used only English.

However, my first observations as well as the first interviews with the focal children's parents, made it clear that even these six 'ESL learners' had a wide variety of pre-school first language and English experience. Knowing that such diversity authentically typified the school's classrooms, I decided to work with this sample of children in observing their language development for the next three years. Because I made no attempt to compare individual competence over time, the fact that the children started from such different baselines did not confound the issue.

Table 1.1 Summary of data collection

Classroom observations	Kindergarten (1994–95)	Grade 1 (1995–96)	Grade 2 (1996–97)
Field notes and audio taping	Morning (regular session)*	Morning (half day)	Morning (1.5 hours)
Video-taping	Once a month	Once a month	Once a month
Teacher interviews	Beginning, middle and end of year	Beginning, middle and end of year	Beginning, middle and end of year
Family interviews	Beginning and end of year	Beginning and end of year	Beginning and end of year

*In addition to the weekly observations, the kindergarten children were observed in the afternoon Language Development session once a month.

My data sources for the study were diverse and Table 1.1 summarises the three years of data collection. In the kindergarten classroom, I observed once a week for a morning and for a whole day once a month. In the Grade 1 classroom, I observed for a morning once a week. When the children were enrolled in Grade 2, I observed once a week during their 1.5 hour Language Arts class. During this Grade 2 year, graduate student researchers Sarah Yip and Elaine Day also conducted observations. Sarah and Elaine observed sometimes on the same day as I did, sometimes on other days.

Throughout, we kept fieldnotes and frequently audio-taped classroom interactions. Simon Fraser University's Faculty of Education video technician, Linda Hof, who had much classroom video-taping experience, video-taped the classrooms at least once a month throughout the three years of the study, for a total of almost 80 hours of video-tape. Research assistants Sarah and Elaine were joined by Lisa Day in transcribing video recordings. These recordings were used as data for analyses. I further used the video-tapes as a triangulation device throughout the write-up of the study. Sarah, Elaine and two other research assistants, Thoko Muthwa-Kuehn and Allyson Julé-Lemke, and I reviewed video-tapes as I completed drafts of chapters and we looked for examples that confirmed or contradicted observations I had made of classroom practices and events.

I interviewed all parents (in English) at the beginning of the study. Bilingual research assistants (Kunwal Aurora, Karen Dhaliwal-Rai, Dr Bozena Karwowska, Sarah Yip and Lanny Young) subsequently interviewed the parents twice each year in their home languages. They also interviewed the children in their homes at the same time so as to record children's use of their home languages.

I interviewed each teacher formally three times during the years. We also discussed matters of interest informally as they came up, during class times, recess, lunch hours, and so on. Research assistants transcribed the tape-recorded teacher interviews.

Research assistants and I transcribed both the audio- and video-tape recordings. I randomly checked transcripts during data analysis, and checked transcripts of all data to be published. In the case of the interviews with parents and children in their home languages, the bilingual research assistants who conducted the interviews made English summaries of them.

I began the analysis of the data collected in the study with respect to the practices by which children came to construct and be assigned identities as school children. Chapter 2 begins that exploration, as I introduce the children and give examples of their interactions in their kindergarten that contributed, I believe, to how they were seen by others there.

Notes

1.   A focus on the politics of social and cultural construction makes the 'naturalness' of social arrangements and constructs problematic. From this perspective, a concept like 'natural communicative language skills' (Strong, 1983), for example, would be investigated with a view to discovering what kinds of communication skills are seen as 'natural'; who do they appear 'natural' for? (and, importantly, who are they seemingly

not 'natural' for?); who makes decisions about the rank of 'skills'; who benefits from the selection of some competencies rather than others for ranking and so on.

2. Wertsch (1991) makes the point that Vygotsky's emphasis on the use of this mediational means may have been because of the particular sociocultural characteristics of his own community, as later research (e.g. Rogoff *et al.*, 1993) have shown less reliance on verbal means in non-European communities.

3. The school, city, teachers and children have been assigned fictitious names to protect their anonymity. Attempts have been made in the case of the children to represent the ethnic identification of their given names.

4. It subsequently became clear that one of the Chinese children (Amy) came from a Cantonese-speaking home, and Teochew was used in the home of the other child (Harvey).

CHAPTER 2

Kindergarten Stories

> We are by this time alive to the fact that inconclusive stories are legitimate; that
> is to say, though they leave us feeling melancholy and perhaps uncertain, yet
> somehow or other they provide a resting point for the mind – a solid object
> casting its shade of reflection and speculation. (Woolf, 1977: 123)

In this chapter, I introduce the kindergarten and each of the six focal children
involved in this research. I include stories about the focal children's kindergarten
experiences not only to introduce them but also to provide ways to talk about how
their identities were constructed by their participation in the activities of their
communities. My data revealed complex and contradictory stories and information
about the children, at least partly because the data came from multiple sources:
parent and teacher interviews and classroom observations. In addition, I observed
these children over the course of their kindergarten year and this, at least minimally
historical information, provided shifting views of who they were and what they did.
And finally, although data principally focused on the children engaged in classroom
practices (and not on their interactions outside of school), this detailed look provides
a sense of how complex classrooms are. In classrooms, children participate in
widely varying activities, with varying participants and mediating means and these
variations also have effects on who they are.

The different perspectives of differently situated observers lead to some-
times-different, sometimes-congruent 'takes' on each child. However, there are
complexities and contradictions within the accounts of single observers and I have
tried to include as much information as possible on each child, making the source of
the information clear. Unless otherwise stated, all the classroom interactional material reported here comes from my observation recorded in fieldnotes, audio-, and
video-tapes.

LIFE IN KINDERGARTEN

The kindergarten classroom, on the west side of the school on the ground floor, faces the playground and beyond that, a busy street. The classroom itself, bright and large, is usually colourfully decorated with the students' art projects and materials pertaining to the classroom themes. The classroom has many well-equipped 'centres': book centre, housekeeping centre, puppet theatre, puzzle centre, computer centre, block centre, sand table, water table, painting easels, listening centre, and so on. The deterioration evident in other parts of the school is not so apparent here: stocked with many of the teacher's personal belongings (a puppet theatre, books, toys and so on, many of which belonged to her own children), the room is inviting, clean and comfortable, although often very hot in the afternoons.

In 1994–95, 19 children were enrolled at the beginning of the year; two children left the class over the course of the year and three children joined it. Mrs Clark, the kindergarten teacher in 1994, had taught kindergarten at Suburban School for two years and had taught for 14 years in total. A speaker of English, she had no specific academic preparation for teaching English as a second language (TESL), but she read TESL professional development materials and attended workshops occasionally. She planned in cooperation with Mrs Smith, who taught another kindergarten class across the hall. Both teachers used and taught the same materials, songs and activities, and their classroom routines were very similar.

During the kindergarten morning, Mrs Clark and her students engaged in: opening circle, 'work', activity time, snack, looking at books, and closing circle. After closing circle, the 11 children who were 'not ESL' were dismissed and went home. The eight remaining children (the minority language background children, whose parents had agreed to an afternoon Language Development class) ate lunches (brought from home) while supervised by a teacher's aide and then played outside for about 15 minutes. Then, the children and Mrs Clark would reassemble in the classroom for the Language Development class, which included children from both Mrs Clark's and Mrs Smith's kindergartens.

The morning routine described above varied somewhat when the children received instruction from other teachers (music, library time) or when Mrs Clark took them to the school gymnasium for physical education. As well, after a school break in April, the children had recess mid-morning with the other children in the school and went outside to the playground for 15 minutes. Otherwise, the structure of the time they spent together was consistent over the year. The routine in the afternoon Language Development class was similar to that of the morning. The themes used in the afternoon were different from morning themes, as were the craft activities ('work'). Mrs Clark judged that she spent more time in the afternoons repeating vocabulary items and focusing on vocabulary development.

On the whole, life in this kindergarten seemed particularly smooth and enjoyable. Most of the children often appeared happy and comfortable there, and much classroom practice seemed explicitly designed to encourage harmony. In interactions involving the teacher, voices were never raised, smiles were frequent and an atmosphere of friendliness and peacefulness prevailed. Mrs Clark reminded children of transgressions of classroom rules quietly and respectfully. As children listened to stories, many of them leaned on one another and stroked each other's hair and clothing. They enthusiastically sang and recited the songs and chants taught to them. Children gave one another and Mrs Clark gifts; they were clearly touched and pleased by the Valentine cards they received from one another. When two children moved away and left the class, Mrs Clark and the children talked about missing them. Affiliations with one another were strong and explicitly articulated. In all, this classroom group felt like a community, with all the positive connotations of the word. Members shared materials, language, rules and other mediating means, and the children learned together to manage these resources.

The kindergarten class contained 11 children (six boys and five girls) who did not use languages other than English. Over the course of the year, though not directly focusing observation on them, I came to know something of their lives in the kindergarten as well. I observed the focal children in large and small group settings, and their interlocutors were sometimes other focal children, but often not. Consequently, the children as a whole (except for one student whose parents refused permission for video-taping) were observed, video-taped and audio-recorded.

I was a uniquely positioned participant in the community of this kindergarten. I had access not only to my observations of the children and the classroom and my interpretations of those observations, but also to some of the teacher's and parents' stories and interpretations. The following selections from the data address the question of what kind of person each child was taken to be and/or became in the context of the kindergarten class. As I mentioned earlier, contradictions between differently situated observers' observations and interpretations, as well as within any observer's observations and interpretations, should not surprise the reader.

More general comments about what kinds of identities appear to be available to children, and what effects having one or another sort of identity might have on access to 'conversations' in the classroom are taken up in detail in Chapter 3. Now, let us meet the children.

THE CHILDREN'S STORIES

Randy

Randy was the oldest child in a Punjabi-speaking family and lived with his father, mother, sister, paternal grandparents, aunt, uncle and adult cousin. Before they entered school, Randy and his sister were cared for by their grandfather, who talked to them in Punjabi. Randy attended an English-medium pre-school programme for 2.5 years. His mother felt he had not made many friends there, except for another Punjabi-speaking child.

Randy's mother reported that the family speaks Punjabi at all times in their home. She thought Randy's Punjabi was good, but by November of his kindergarten year she felt that he was learning English well too. Karin Dhaliwal-Rai, who conducted many of the Punjabi home interviews, reported after her first meeting with Randy in January of his kindergarten year, that he pronounced Punjabi well and he appeared comfortable and fluent speaking it. She noticed some English words in Randy's Punjabi speech, mostly for vocabulary items from school and child popular culture domains. His parents also reported to Karin that they had noticed more English words in his Punjabi speech since he had started kindergarten. They also reported that Randy replied in Punjabi to older cousins who addressed him in English; they thought that he practised speaking English with his younger sister but not with other family members.

Randy was initially silent upon his entry to kindergarten; when questioned by Mrs Clark or other adults, he rarely answered. Nor did Randy appear to seek out interaction with other children: the activities in which he chose to engage at school until about the end of November (puzzles and colouring pictures) did not require other children's participation. Even when children played beside him, he did not verbally interact with them. I never heard Randy speak in Punjabi to any of the Punjabi-speaking children. Nevertheless, when fieldwork began, Randy appeared attentive to the English stories Mrs Clark read and apparently enjoyed the repetitive songs and chants of 'circle' time.

In November of Randy's kindergarten year, I interviewed his mother (with the school district's Punjabi-speaking home-school worker interpreting) for the first time. We spoke about her perceptions of her son. She thought that he was very shy (in her words, 'just like his father') but that he was happy to be going to kindergarten and seemed to be adjusting well to school. She also thought that he was learning a good deal there. In January, research assistant Karin Dhaliwal-Rai interviewed his mother. This excerpt from Karin's English interpretation of their conversation concerns Randy's reactions to what he was learning at school:

(1)

> Whenever he learns a song, he comes home and tells her [his mother] about it and repeats it over and over again and also the other lessons too, he will come home and share it with her. Whenever he is in the car, he sings all the songs he has learned at school. When they are travelling in the car, he prefers to have English music on compared to Punjabi music.

Randy's mother also spoke of her perception of her son's desire to do well in school. Karin interpreted his mother's words:

(2)

> He wants to learn really fast what's going on. So when he doesn't do something on task, he kind of feels upset about it. Like for instance when he colours and it

goes outside the line he will be upset at himself, oh gosh why is this happening, why aren't I learning. So it's kind of hard on him. Sometimes he will get this sad look on his face and he will say why didn't I get it and sometimes he'll get upset. He will just sit in one little spot and he will do it again, he will start his work again.

Noting that she and her husband hoped Randy would get a good education and a good job, Randy's mom mentioned that his father 'sometimes encourages him to speak more English, like, I will get you this if you try to speak more'.

Mrs Clark was worried about Randy in early November. Though she was pleased with his near-perfect attendance record, she found his continued silence in the classroom a concern and she told me on 15 November she planned to refer him for assessment to the school district's psychological services.[1]

However, later in November, Randy's participation in some aspects of kindergarten appeared to increase. His mother had mentioned Randy's repetition of school songs at home. Seating himself almost always right next to Mrs Clark at circle time, a practice he continued throughout the year, in November he smiled and looked increasingly comfortable during choral songs and speech. It appeared to me in some way that the songs and chants of the circle 'seduced' Randy into voice. Beginning with some tension around his lips, then minimal and finally full participation, Randy moved to become a participant in the 'choir' of the circle. This participation did not, of course, mean that Randy took on the position of soloist right away; his solo verbal performances in front of the large group remained minimal until later in the year.

Mrs Clark often 'scaffolded' Randy's verbal participation in classroom activities.[2] At the end of November, she approached Randy as he was colouring a picture of the 'three bears'.

(3)

Mrs Clark:	Who's this?
Randy:	(*quietly*) Papa
Mrs Clark:	What does papa bear say?
	Randy looks at Mrs Clark.
Mrs Clark:	Who:'s (*rising intonation – over to you*)
Randy:	Who's (*pause 4 seconds*) [been
Mrs Clark:	[sitting in my chair?[3]

Mrs Clark commonly collaborated with Randy in completion of a turn at the circle as well, in much the same way. After one of these collaborations, after completion of the 'task', she would praise him warmly.

In December, a child sitting next to Randy, as well as the teacher, scaffolded his participation:

(4)

Group doing a counting game with cards. Each card has a large number on it as well as a small one. Randy's card says 17 12

Lisa:	Who has 17?
	Randy looks at his card.
Earl:	*(whispering)*: I have 17.
Randy:	I have 17.
Mrs Clark:	Who::: has *(rising intonation)*
Randy:	20
Mrs Clark:	12.

In January, the children played this game again using cards with alphabet letters. At the end of the month, when Randy's turn came, he said with no hesitation: 'I have T, who have L?'

Even near the end of the year, his teacher still often scaffolded Randy's contributions:

(5)

Mrs Clark:	Anything to share, Randy?
	Randy shakes his head.
	Let me see your smile, Randy. When you said good morning to me, I saw a tooth gone. When did that fall out?
Randy:	When I was sleeping.
Mrs Clark:	Last night?
	Randy nods.
	Oh wow. Did you find it on your pillow?
	Randy shakes his head.
	You didn't swallow it? Where was it this morning?
	(Pause 7 seconds)
	Did you swallow it?
	I thought I saw a new smile. So you <u>did</u> have something to share with us.
	She smiles.

Randy's mother's description of his habits of persistence with tasks was evident in a November observation. On that occasion, Randy spent about 30 minutes working on an alphabet puzzle. He got A–F attached and then began a long, partly random, partly rational strategy for completing the puzzle, which I described in fieldnotes:

(6)

Randy getting the alphabet puzzle, gets A–F done right away. Tries J, knows it's not right, tries W, P, R, I, U. His hand is on G, but he doesn't pick it up. Tries P again. Attaches O to P. Tries S on F. Tries X. Tries G, it works, goes immediately to H, then I. Tries to attach O and P. Tries Y, R. Then goes back, points to A and sings (sotto voce), A, B, C, D, E, F, G, H, I. Stops. Goes to puzzle box and studies it to see what comes after I. (It's hard to see.) Gets J. I (KT) point out the wall alphabet to him, I say: Will that help? *No answer. He gets K and L, then stops. Sings from beginning again. Gets as far as Q. (Several more trial and error and singing attempts until he finishes – takes about 10 minutes from beginning.)*

Mrs Clark comes up: Did you do all that, Randy? Can you say it to me? Nice and loud. *He does, but I can't hear it (she does).*

Randy's efforts to solve this puzzle and his reliance on the tools of the box and the song to aid in this problem illustrated a repeated pattern of persisting with school-defined tasks, managing his actions privately and quietly.

Beginning in late November and continuing throughout the year, Randy increased his verbal contributions in the kindergarten. Mrs Clark reported in the middle of November that Randy had said quietly to her, 'I can't glue it', the first sentential utterance she had heard from him since beginning school. Near the end of November, Randy, in play with Harvey, said 'It's over in the trees'. This was the first time I had heard him say anything in kindergarten. Increasingly, when called upon in the circle time, Randy would respond to the teacher's performance-oriented questions with one word answers (e.g. to questions like, 'What colour is it? What shape is this?'). In early January, Randy volunteered an answer to a teacher prompt: In the context of writing a class poem about winter, in which Mrs Clark had provided several examples of the sort: 'Winter is snow; winter is not swim suits'.[4] Randy volunteered 'Winter is boots; winter is not a pumpkin'.

Randy was slower to interact with the other children than with Mrs Clark; he began to interact with Harvey and Martin (other focal children) in late January. Much of this conversation occurred in play with some dinosaur models, in which many of the boys were interested. Typically, such interactions included handling the models, bashing models into other models, vocalisations of crashing noises and utterances like 'He's killing your guy; You're dead' and so on. Randy actively participated in this interaction and showed real pleasure in it. He continued to play with the dinosaur models into April, by which time the other boys apparently had lost interest in them. During this time, Randy continued his action and talk with the dinosaurs very quietly and mostly by himself.

At the end of January, Randy brought some hockey trading cards to show at 'Sharing Time', the first time he had brought anything to show. His verbal contribution on this occasion was: 'I got them at the store – hockey cards.' Mrs Clark extended his turn by asking him if he watched hockey and if he had favourites among his cards. Randy responded to these initiations non-verbally. In April, Randy participated in a very common interactional pattern in the classroom in which he had not participated previously. As the children coloured pictures, they often chatted among themselves about what they were colouring, what colours they were using, or topics unrelated to the present activity. On 18 April, the following conversation took place:

(7)

Randy and Abe and Morgan colouring pictures. Morgan calls out, 'No King, no king, la la la la la la [a phrase from the movie The Lion King]

Randy:	*(smiles broadly, then darts away)* I need yellow! *(looking at picture on puzzle of Simba, checking colour?)*
Abe:	*(looking at Morgan's picture)* Oh yuck.
Morgan:	That's supposed to be yuck.
Randy:	*(to Morgan)* You need the brown.
Morgan:	Yeah.
Randy:	I like red.
Abe:	I like red.
Morgan:	You both like red. I hate red.
Randy:	I like white.
Abe:	Me too.
Morgan:	Me too.

Randy's active involvement and initiative in this conversation, simple as it was, did not resemble his previous participation in the classroom. Here, he told someone else what he needed, expressed a preference, had his statements listened to, and he agreed and disagreed with other students. From this time to the end of the school year, Randy increasingly participated more and more actively in classroom conversations like this and others. He initiated conversations with other children, displayed his knowledge (30 May: Randy *(to me)*: 'I know how to spell dog. D-O-G!'), and participated in imaginative play. Increasingly, Randy began to direct communicative efforts toward Earl, one of the more powerful-appearing boys in the kindergarten.

Possibly because Randy began the year so silently, his increasing participation in classroom activities seemed to surprise his teacher somewhat. Several times when Randy answered a question correctly, or performed well, Mrs Clark's positive response indicated (to my ears, anyway) some element of surprise. For example, during a video-taped encounter on 7 February, when Mrs Clark asked the children individually to select the first, the third, and so on from a series of hearts displayed in a pocket chart, Randy volunteered to select the seventh.

(8)

Randy goes to chart and quickly removes the seventh heart.

Mrs Clark:	Wow. He didn't even count. How did you know that was the seventh?
	She smiles at Randy.
	Randy says nothing.

Did you count them?
Randy says nothing.
No? You just knew that was where 7 would be?
Randy nods almost imperceptibly.
Good for you.

During an interview in February, Mrs Clark echoed her assessment of Randy's 'surprising' abilities in comparison to anglophone students.

(9)

> I look at kids like Melanie (an anglophone student) and she looks very good, but then I assess her and compare her with kids like Randy and she's way behind. If these white English-speaking parents knew this they'd be some upset. You look at the scholarship winners in this school district and they're all kids who used to be ESL.

This statement included the interesting notion that one's identity as 'ESL' could shift – one could, in a sense, graduate from 'ESL kid' to being a scholarship winner.

Randy's mother's November report of his disinterest in Punjabi was echoed in a conversation I had with a group of children, including Randy, at the end of April. A child at another table said something in Polish. Morgan (who joined the kindergarten in January and whose family used Polish at home) began the conversation.

(10)

Morgan:	*(to me)* Do you know how to talk that language?
KT:	No, I only know how to talk English, I'm not as smart as you. I don't know how to talk Polish or Punjabi or Chinese like you kids.
Randy:	Earl speaks Chinese.
KT:	And you know Punjabi.
Randy:	No.
KT:	Did you forget?
	Randy nods.

In January, Karin Dhaliwal-Rai interviewed Randy and his parents in their home. Although Karin judged that he spoke fluent Punjabi and that his pronunciation was very good (his parents concurred), Karin interpreted Randy's mother's remarks:

(11)

> Randy does not like to watch Punjabi/Hindi movies on video. Randy said that his teacher told him only to watch cartoons and English movies but no Indian movies. Randy also tells them (his parents) that this is why they have not learned English because they watch Indian movies. He will leave the room if they watch them.

In addition, Karin reported that Randy clearly said that he did not like Punjabi and discouraged his parents from participating in Punjabi events. Mrs Clark told me that she had initially counselled the children not to speak their first languages in school and to watch English television; however, after reading some literature on teaching ESL, in November she had contradicted this directive and told them that they were free to speak their first languages in school and that those languages were important.[5]

Randy came into kindergarten as a quiet boy who persisted at school tasks. He did not miss any days of school throughout the year. Initially, at least his teacher and perhaps his parents, saw his silence as potentially problematic. However, Randy's silence in school 'broke' at a most auspicious time. He was not assessed as requiring 'learning assistance' and he became increasingly able to participate in conversations with classmates of his choice. His classroom presented him with mediating means he liked: the songs, the chants and the dinosaurs. His teacher evaluated his persistence positively. The verbal scaffolds other children and his teacher gave him successfully 'held his place' for him. Mrs Clark frequently praised him. At the end of the year, Mrs Clark wrote on his report card: 'I am pleased with Randy's increasing confidence this year'. His report card also reflected her perception that Randy's growing competence in literacy would do much to ensure his success in school. At the same time, Randy's proficiency in Punjabi was not a part of his definition as a 'successful schoolboy'.

Surjeet

Surjeet was the oldest of three children in her Punjabi-speaking family. Surjeet's grandparents, who had been teachers (her grandfather, a school administrator too) in India, also lived with her family; in addition, an aunt and two older cousins lived in the ground-floor apartment of Surjeet's house. Before entering school, she had been cared for either by one of her parents, her aunt, or by her grandparents, while her parents worked outside the home. All these adults could speak both Punjabi and English. Her mother reported that the adults in Surjeet's home communicated in Punjabi,[6] that adults spoke to children in a mixture of Punjabi and English, but that the children usually conversed in English among themselves and usually answered adults in English. In November 1994, Surjeet's mother said she felt that Surjeet understood Punjabi reasonably well but Surjeet couldn't really speak it ('A few words she speaks, but she cannot make a sentence') and was primarily an English speaker. Her mother reported to me that Surjeet was a 'late talker' (she had not started to speak until age 3) and that she wondered whether Surjeet's language development might have been delayed because Surjeet was 'shy' (a characteristic adult relatives attributed to Surjeet several times), or because she played so much with older children (her cousins) who might have 'spoken for' her. On another occasion, Surjeet's grandfather told Karin Dhaliwal-Rai that after she became fluent in English, he would teach Surjeet Punjabi. I never observed Surjeet speaking Punjabi or playing with children who were speaking Punjabi at school.[7]

Karin Dhaliwal-Rai interviewed Surjeet in her home in January and June of her kindergarten year, in an attempt to assess her Punjabi proficiency. On both occasions, she found it difficult to engage Surjeet in extended conversation. Karin concluded that Surjeet understood Punjabi fairly well for a Canadian child her age, but spoke it only rudimentarily. She could repeat a prayer said by the family every day, after a good deal of scaffolding from her mother, and was able to understand questions put to her in Punjabi. When Karin addressed her in Punjabi, she usually answered in English; if pressed, she would use a few Punjabi words in a primarily English sentence. Karin summarised her observations about Surjeet's Punjabi use:

(12)

Surjeet does not get read to in Punjabi and is not encouraged to read or write in Punjabi, as she is in English, but she is still getting other forms of exposure to Punjabi in her life. One form is through audio-cassettes of Bhangra, Punjabi dance music. There was one Bhangra tape in her home that was a favourite of all the children, including Surjeet. Surjeet's grandmother said when these tapes are played, the kids enjoy dancing around to the music . . . . The other form of Punjabi that is in Surjeet's life takes the form of media, 'RimJim', the 24-hour Hindi/Punjabi radio. It seems 'RimJim' is always on in this household. The radio daily presents Punjabi songs, on the air open talk shows, Sikh prayers and the news in Punjabi.

Mrs Clark stated in October that she thought Surjeet was 'really shy and withdrawn' and that Surjeet played by herself most of the time. She mentioned that Surjeet had had no pre-school programme and had had a difficult time separating from her mother in the first week of school. She wondered whether Surjeet had a 'learning problem', but was unsure:

(13)

When I consider where she was – she couldn't even recognise her name in the beginning and now she's writing it without a model, she's coming, and yet in other respects she's so low, like in counting one to ten, she really doesn't get it. So we'll have to see.

Mrs Clark's uncertainty about Surjeet's academic abilities persisted throughout the year, but she ceased to worry about Surjeet's social isolation, because very quickly Surjeet and Donna (an anglophone girl) began to play together, and Surjeet also participated actively in conversations with other children. Her close association with Donna lasted until about April, after which time the two girls played together only occasionally. Indeed, after that association became less strong, Surjeet did not play with any one child in particular. Although she did play with a variety of other children, as the year was coming to an end she spent more time in the classroom alone.

Although several members of her family (and initially, her teacher) reported that Surjeet was 'shy' and she certainly displayed 'shyness' on some occasions,[8] Surjeet from the beginning of the research talked and interacted with many other children. However, although she was sometimes attentive to the songs, rhymes and chants of the circle, she rarely participated in 'solo' turns (answering teacher questions, volunteering information and so on).

Surjeet paid strikingly little attention to the stories Mrs Clark read to the children, and sometimes even to directions Mrs Clark gave for completion of tasks. Almost every day, Mrs Clark read a story to the children as they sat on the carpet; as she began, the 'circle' collapsed, as the children moved closer to her so they could see the book's pictures. At such times, if Surjeet had initially been close to Mrs Clark in the circle, in the rearrangement, another child moving in would take Surjeet's place, or she would place herself at the outside edges of the circle. There she would very obviously occupy herself with matters other than the story: she might look around the classroom, stroke another child, finger her bracelet and/or move from place to place on the floor. During kindergarten, I never saw Surjeet attend except very briefly to a story read aloud. When the other children responded emotionally to events in the stories, with groans or laughs, for example, she would come to attention, look at her classmates, and sometimes her expressions would mirror theirs. At such times, she appeared to attend not to the story, but rather, to her classmates. Mrs Clark also noticed that Surjeet did not appear engaged whenever the children viewed a video-tape.

Surjeet's behaviour during a video-tape presentation near the end of the year led me to wonder whether her inattention was selective or general. The video-tape, an episode of the American television programme 'Reading Rainbow', started with a narrated reading of a storybook (with accompanying illustrations) about a whale. During the story reading, Surjeet moved to seven different locations, looked around, whispered to other children, and looked at the ceiling. Near the end of the programme, the video showed several children giving their reviews of the book. For this part of the video, Surjeet sat very still, gazed toward the television screen and looked attentive.

Surjeet often appeared almost hyper-attentive to other children and sometimes to Mrs Clark; in such cases, her comprehension and expertise appeared quite keen. The video-taped records clearly show Surjeet's intent gaze toward children who were speaking during 'Circle Time' as well as her obvious attention to other children at the tables during work time. Her rapt attention to other children sometimes seemed counterproductive to her completion of the set tasks. On several occasions, Surjeet began one of the craft projects and then became apparently confused as she noticed other children doing these projects in a variety of ways. Concerned about doing things correctly, she seemed to find this diversity confusing and she would revise what she was doing on the basis of her observations of others.

Doing things correctly appeared a primary concern of Surjeet's. She often gave directions to other children (and once to me)[9]. These directions commonly took the form of reminding other children of a classroom rule or a ventriloquation of a teacher directive (e.g. Surjeet *(to Mitch)*: You need to cut it out!; Surjeet *(to Martin)*: Put away your backpack!) Although she gave many directions, it would be inaccurate to portray Surjeet as a powerful child whose directions the others always heeded. On the contrary, many children commonly ignored her directives. For example:

(14)

Amy and Cathy at sand table. Surjeet comes up.

Surjeet: You can't have water!
Cathy: Who cares?

They ignore Surjeet.

I surmised that the other girls defined Surjeet's directive as irrelevant either because they didn't have water anyway or because they dismissed Surjeet's right to tell them what to do. On the other hand, Surjeet sometimes could command the attention of two classmates, Martin and Harvey (in examples to be discussed later), when she issued directives to them. Sometimes they resisted her directives, but they did apparently listen to them.

Other children's responses to Surjeet's conversational gambits appeared connected with this matter of ignoring or resisting Surjeet's directives. Again, the evidence is contradictory. Sometimes Surjeet actively participated in conversations with other children, especially during the first half of the year. An example is this interaction in January with Melanie:

(15)

Surjeet and Melanie are at water table.

Surjeet: This is a flower thing.
Melanie: This is soap.
                 Girls cooperating in filling things.
                 Thank you, Surjeet. How do you make bubbles?
Surjeet: You press it <u>hard</u>.
Melanie: Put some more in here, Surjeet. That's enough. You water the garden while I get some nice good stuff.
Surjeet: More?
Melanie: A <u>little</u> more in there.
Surjeet: A little more? *(offers water)*
Melanie: No.
Surjeet: You're not playing?
Melanie: Yes.

Surjeet: *(notices her sleeves are wet).* Oh-oh. My mom will hit me. *(Not distressed, part of the companionship.)*

Girls stop and dry their hands.

Such friendly, imaginative and relatively cooperative[10] play was sometimes evident in interactions with Surjeet in the playhouse – a centre to which she tried often for access. The classroom rule was that four children only were allowed in the playhouse (other centres had different quotas); although Surjeet often wanted to get in there, she didn't always manage it, because other children might complete their craft project faster than her, install themselves and invite others there before Surjeet was free.

As the year wore on, Surjeet more frequently made conversational contributions that appeared internally contradictory or which other children did not take up. Consider this conversation in April:

(16)

Donna, Surjeet and Melanie colouring pictures of Easter eggs and ducks and rabbits.

Donna: That's not supposed to be pink. *(to Surjeet regarding her duck, which she has coloured pink)*

Surjeet: Meagan, Mitch is using the sparkles. Randy too. Melanie, go tell Mrs Clark.

Melanie: Ryan was too. I'm shocked.

Donna: I'm too.

Surjeet: My dog lives in my house, he bites me, no he doesn't bite me.

Amy: *(to Surjeet re her pink Easter egg)* This a yours?
Amy picks it up. Surjeet is upset.

Surjeet: Leave it.

Amy: OK. *(She puts it down)*

Donna: I have 3 or 4 *(Easter eggs)* from Katy's party *(gestures to picture).*

Surjeet: Me too. I have 10 hundred. I can't go to people's birthday parties.

Although conversations accompanying colouring were commonly somewhat free-wheeling, not very coherent or cohesive, the other children neither heeded Surjeet's direction to go tell Mrs Clark[11] nor took up her contradictory contribution about her dog. Although some of them began the year using phrases like '10 hundred', by this time, most of the children were using plausible-sounding numbers in their contributions and enforcing others' use of such numbers. They sometimes mocked younger children who persisted in using number constructions they did not recognise as 'right'. Hence I suspect they noted Surjeet's use of the improbable number, even though they did not remark upon it in subsequent conversation.

In February, while Surjeet was gluing pieces of paper to two toilet paper rolls, Nina approached her:

(17)

Nina:	What are you making?
Surjeet:	A phone. *(She looks up at Nina)*
Nina:	What kind of phone? What kind of phone? *(Pause 5 seconds)*
Surjeet:	It's not a phone.
Nina:	Then why do you need that red paper?
Surjeet:	*(glances at red paper)* It's not, it's a pur: *(eyes widen)* I don't need it! I only need /dIs/ *(gestures to white paper beside her)*
Nina:	Then why did you get that red paper?
Surjeet:	I didn't do it. Randy got it.
Nina:	I don't believe you.
Surjeet:	I saw ****
Nina:	I didn't even just see Randy on this table.
Surjeet:	I sitted here! *(eyes widen and she gestures to chair beside her)*
Nina:	Well, he's *(Randy's)* on that table. *(gestures to the table where Randy is sitting.)*
Surjeet:	****
Nina:	I know everything
Surjeet:	No you don't.
Nina:	Yes I do.
Surjeet:	No you don't.
Nina:	*(singing)* I know everything. I know everything. *Julie approaches.*
Julie:	*(to Surjeet)* What are you making?
Nina:	Julie, Julie, what did the cat do?
Julie:	I don't know. I don't know.

She walks away. Nina also leaves.

In this conversation, Nina badgered Surjeet about the red paper, saying she does not believe Surjeet. Surjeet asserted initially she was making a phone and then contradicted that assertion.[12] The interaction ended with Nina telling Surjeet that she (Nina) 'knows everything' and usurping Surjeet's turn in the conversation after Julie asked Surjeet a question. This attempt to position Surjeet as *not* knowing everything (which Surjeet resisted mildly), as not believed and as not allowed a conversational place, became a relatively common practice in the classroom. Surjeet's sometimes non-cohesive conversational contributions seemed part of this process – she did not seem able to find a place for herself easily within conversations.

However, in some conversations Surjeet's utterances did seem tied one to others, for example this conversation in June:

(18)

Children are writing the alphabet and drawing pictures at the table.

Surjeet:	I'm not scribbling like Harvey. Look, I'm not scribbling like Harvey.
Mitch:	Harvey always scribbles. Every time I sit beside him.
Surjeet:	Yeah.
	Harvey comes over. They watch him.
Surjeet:	See he's scribbling.
Mitch:	No he's not.
Surjeet:	I have a friend outside who scribbles like Harvey.
	Mrs Clark comes over.
	See, I'm not scribbling like Harvey.
Mrs Clark:	Harvey doesn't scribble anymore. He's learned how to do it right.

The conversation continues as children colour. Surjeet continues to discuss scribbling.

This conversation continued for some time, during which time Surjeet accused Harvey of being a 'copycatter' for using the chart on the wall to get his alphabet right and Surjeet told me that 'I didn't look at that [the chart], I just knowed it! I'm not scribbling!' Surjeet here participated in the positioning of Harvey as incompetent and attempted to distance herself from such incompetence. Again, we see Surjeet's concern with doing things correctly.

In fact, Surjeet did do a lot correctly in her classroom and her efforts in this regard were considerable. Much of this expertise centred around literacy activities. In February, she delivered all her Valentine cards, which involved matching the names she had written on the envelopes of her cards to the names the children had put on the outside of mailboxes they had constructed. This was more difficult than it sounds, because the formation of the names addressed by the senders, often differed considerably from the formation of the names on the mailboxes of the receivers. Surjeet interrupted her own deliveries several times to point out mailboxes for which other children were looking. After she finished her own deliveries, she offered to help Donna, who was obviously having trouble with the task. In the midst of helping Donna, with several children milling about the mailboxes, Surjeet also gave assistance to other children. Her assistance looked very efficient and accurate. The video-tape that shows Surjeet doing this matching also shows Randy engaged in the same exercise. Randy glanced briefly at the names on his cards, tried somewhat half-heartedly to find matches, and then put the cards in the mailboxes one by one starting on the left, without regard for the names on the envelopes or the names on the mailboxes. The contrast with Surjeet was striking. Earlier in the year, I observed Surjeet with two other children playing a Concentration game with alphabet letters on cards. Surjeet handily won the game. She then continued to play with other children, winning each time. In March, as she examined a chart with children's names on it, Surjeet remarked to Mrs Clark: 'Abe's got a small name!' She also approached Mrs Clark on another occasion in March, pointing to the label on Mrs Clark's desk: 'I can read this! "Mrs Clark's desk!"' Her numeracy abilities also apparently developed over the course of the year. As Mrs Clark had noted, Surjeet did not participate in the choral chanting of numbers in the circle at the beginning of the year. However, video-tapes taken in May sometimes show her leading the group in choral counting. In addition, her paintings were detailed and colourful. But her expertise in these activities did not seem part of 'what everybody knew' about her.

Near the end of the year, an incident in the library provided me a metaphor for thinking about Surjeet. Surjeet was sitting on a chair at a table in the library and Julie came up to her saying '*I* have to sit somewhere'. Julie then bent her knees and put her hips down on the side of Surjeet's chair, forcing Surjeet out. Surjeet did not protest this, and she moved to another chair in the library. Earlier in the year, I had seen similar incidents:

(19)

Surjeet sitting in Mrs Clark's chair in the circle. Oscar approaches.

Oscar: I want to sit there.
Surjeet: I was sitting here first.
               Melanie approaches.
Melanie: Surjeet, leave.

Surjeet leaves and Oscar sits down. Surjeet goes to plasticine table.

On several occasions, children took materials that Surjeet was using out of her hands, or she gave up materials when they demanded them. In addition, many times Surjeet stood at the entrance to the 'housekeeping' centre, a centre she appeared to really like, but stayed outside, watching other children play. Apparently she had a hard time finding a secure, central, active, and desirable place for herself in this community. It would be incorrect to say she didn't have a place, or that she was marginal to the action; rather, she was there, but her place, her position, could be threatened or taken, and she could be disbelieved and/or ignored.

At the end of the year, Mrs Clark believed that Surjeet was still quite handicapped by incomplete knowledge of English. She recommended to the next year's teacher that Surjeet get extra instruction in ESL. Mrs Clark was also concerned that Surjeet might have a 'Learning Disability' and that she should be tested in Grade 1 for possible remedial placement.

Martin

Martin was born in Germany to Polish-speaking parents who had left Poland and immigrated to Canada when Martin was a year and a half old. As infants, he and his younger brother had attended part-time an English-medium daycare centre for some time while their parents were engaged in educational upgrading in Canada; after this, one or other of their parents cared for them. Martin's family had no other extended family members in Canada, but they were friendly with other Polish-speaking families who lived in their townhouse complex. By the time Martin began kindergarten, his parents had noticed him 'mixing words' of Polish and English: '[He] can say a sentence half Polish, half English. Especially colours, animals, numbers, [he] says it in English'. Dr Bozena Karwowska, the Polish–English bilingual research assistant in this project, assessed Martin's Polish skills in February and June of his kindergarten year. In February, she found Martin's Polish skills quite good:

(20)

> He has no problems with understanding and speaking Polish. In general, he does not mix Polish and English words. He declines nouns and adjectives. His declension of nouns is fairly good. His Polish vocabulary is quite good. In general my impression was that Martin's language is not much lower than the level that is expected from Polish children of his age.

On his entry to kindergarten, Mrs Clark saw Martin as an active and potentially somewhat difficult student; in October, she reported that she had found him 'quite a handful' at the beginning of the school year and had been in touch with his parents about his behaviour. In his father's words in November:

(21)

> At the beginning the teacher was complaining because he was, there are other Polish children and he knows them and the teacher said they were trying, they didn't listen to her, they were just – Martin tried to turn others' attention to himself so he did all kinds of different things, sticking the tongue out and not listening to the teacher, doing all different things. But now the teacher said you have to stay in contact, I will inform you how he is doing, because he has to listen to me because I want to teach him something. If he won't listen to me he won't learn and so we explained it to him a thousand times. I think there is no more problem.

Because fieldwork began in October, I did not see Martin engaging in the behaviours that had initially caused Mrs Clark's communication with his parents. By the time I began to observe, Mrs Clark believed, as did his father, that Martin had 'calmed down' and that his behaviour was acceptable. Nevertheless, Martin's behaviour was consistently an issue throughout the year, particularly for other students.

Striking were numerous instances in which Martin was directed by other children. They told him where to sit, how to complete his work, that he was doing something wrong and so on. Both anglophone and bilingual children gave him directives. In some cases, these directives were offered in a friendly and collusive manner, as when Earl told him in a whisper one day in June when Martin joined the circle with an object for sharing that 'It's girls' day', and Martin secretly put his toy away. At other times, children 'tattled' on Martin to the teacher (e.g. Mark: 'Mrs Clark, Martin's lying down!'), or gave Martin directives in ways that did not appear so collaborative, like Wesley's in June:

(22)

Martin has come and shown Wesley an animal.

Wesley:	Martin, put that back! It's not playtime for you.
	Martin puts it on the track.
	But you're not allowed to put it on the track. It's NOT PLAYTIME FOR YOU. *(loud and slow)*
KT:	Why?
Wesley:	Because he hasn't showed his work *[to Mrs Clark]*.

Wesley often told Martin what to do. On one occasion, while I was watching at a table, and Martin had left to get some materials, Wesley whispered to me 'I have to tell you something but it's a secret. Martin talks rude'. When I asked him what he meant, he said he couldn't say, but he repeated his 'secret' to Julie and Cathy.

Surjeet also provided Martin with many directives. On an occasion in November:

(23)

Surjeet:	Don't, Martin, sit on my chair! *(dramatically)* You're doing it wrong!
	Oh-oh, you need to write your name!
Martin:	But I <u>write</u> my name.

On this occasion, Martin contradicted Surjeet's assumption that he had not written his name on his paper. Such countering of others' commands was not particularly usual for Martin. More typically he acquiesced, as in this encounter:

(24)

Harvey and Martin playing with Brio [wooden trains]. Tim comes over.

Harvey:	Tim. Get out. Get <u>out</u>.
	Harvey and Martin trying to balance bridge.
	Hey, Martin, don't do it. I'm trying to figure this out.

Martin stops and watches Harvey. He waits very patiently.

On another occasion, Martin was playing with some other children in the blocks area, and they built a high tower with blocks. Several children outside the area became distressed about this, and Wesley, in particular, admonished Martin loudly and began to take blocks off the tower. Martin was himself upset with Wesley's reprimand and with the dismantling of the tower; he appealed to Mrs Clark. Mrs Clark restated the classroom rule (no bricks higher than your head) and told Martin: 'Measure to your head, Martin, these friends are helping you'.

Martin usually complied with other students' directives but he sometimes resisted (as in his protest to Surjeet noted above). His resistance to others' directives, including the teacher's or other adults occurred particularly with directives to stop or change activity when he was engaged in colouring, drawing, cutting things out or making something. Like Randy, Martin was persistent but his persistence was evaluated differently from Randy's. It sometimes caused difficulty for him: on several occasions, Mrs Clark or his classmates reminded Martin when he did not make transitions to new activities when so directed.

Martin also resisted somewhat classroom directives about using his first language. At the beginning of the year, the only Polish speakers in the kindergarten were Martin and Julie; in January, Morgan, a Polish-speaking boy, joined the class. Early in the year, Martin spoke quite a bit of Polish to Julie and to two Polish-speaking boys in the afternoon Language Development class, although his parents reported that he had told them that Mrs Clark had said, 'No Polish in school, only English'. Although the rule changed and Mrs Clark stated that the children could uses their first languages, like many of the children Martin spoke his first language less and less over the course of the year or spoke it more surreptitiously. In some cases, children themselves enforced the initial first language ban. In March, Abe (in whose home Kurdish was used), an anglophone girl, Julie and Martin were playing in the puppet centre. Martin had on a duck sock puppet and said something in Polish. Abe replied, 'That's not talking!' Martin then switched to English.

Reasons for code-switching were, of course, bound up with the children's social relations. Martin spoke Polish with Julie and with a frequent playmate, John, in the afternoon class. Children from other language backgrounds sometimes would join these Polish-speaking dyads, and Polish speakers would then switch to English. In the following interaction, Martin switched to English to reprimand Harvey, but he resumed speaking Polish before Harvey left the area:

(25)

> *Martin and John speaking Polish in blocks area.*
> *Harvey comes in – wiggling their tower.*
> *Martin notices and yells:* 'Hey! Stop that, you are wrecking it!'
> *Martin resumes speaking Polish to John. Harvey watches and then leaves.*

Martin was active in the kind of 'side talk', accompanying the completing of crafts, in which most of the anglophone children engaged. He also engaged in imaginative play with other children with blocks, the trains, the puppets and the dinosaurs. In many of these interactions, the other children seemed to value his presence and the interactions were comfortable and peaceful. In the following conversation, while completing a craft centred on the song 'I Know An Old Woman Who Swallowed a Fly', Martin did not notice the shaming attempt by Morgan and another two boys:

(26)

Martin:	If somebody swallowed a fly, that would feel gross. You know what? My dad said that Chinese people eat frogs.
Amy:	You know, my dad eat snake.
Julie:	That would hurt a stomach. Some of the dads and mom eat the snake. Some of the dads kill the snake and cut it and then give it to the children.
Martin:	If you eat frogs, their stomachs will go *(gestures up and down)*
Amy:	I don't eat snake, I just eat sandwich.
	Morgan and two other boys come over to table, gesture to Martin's picture and make some vocalisations like 'Oh-oh, he's doing this wrong'. *Martin doesn't apparently notice. They leave.*
Julie:	Oh-oh. Morgan just said shut up.
Martin:	He's in very deep trouble if he just said shut up. 'Aw, shut up!' *(as if quoting)*

Martin's confident '<u>He's</u> in very deep trouble . . . (my emphasis) seemed to be the remark of someone who, for once, did not fear that he himself was in deep trouble.

Another apparently enjoyable conversation was this:

(27)

*Randy, Ryan and Martin playing with dinosaurs. Making lots of sibilant noises –
Martin knocks down all of Randy's dinosaurs.*

Randy:	Hey! *(not irritated, more amused)*
	All of them bamming into each other's dinosaurs. Gleeful smiles.
Ryan:	*(pretend concern)*: You can't hurt the baby. You gotta protect the egg. We're all buddies on this side.
Martin:	And here's! He's going out in the deep water. He's going on his head.
	Martin and Ryan are ganging up on Randy's dinosaurs.
Ryan:	Bullseye!
Martin:	Bullseye!

After the interaction above, Mrs Clark gently scolded Martin for not stopping his play when she directed all the children to stop and clean up in preparation for recess. She defined Martin's persistence as mis-behaviour.

Martin's contributions, especially in the circle but also sometimes in conversations with peers, often included attempts to communicate fairly sophisticated meanings, despite his beginner's syntax. In a conversation with an anglophone girl in March, Martin was aggrieved because he had only one cupcake holder and the girl had more:

(28)

Martin: You got some lots. It's not to behave some lots. I need some – you got lots of.

The girl did not give up any of her cupcake holders as a result of Martin's reproach, to which she did not respond in any discernible way. Martin made many other attempts to express complicated meanings. Sometimes his interlocutors could easily comprehend his contributions, sometimes they could not. In February, at circle time, Mrs Clark was surprised by how rapidly a girl answered a question:

(29)

Mrs Clark: How did you figure that out so quickly? Did you guess?
Natalie: No.
Martin: Maybe she thought!

In January, when the children had put on a variety of hats indicating different occupations, and then had individually to think up phrases appropriate to that occupation, Martin suggested to the child wearing a crown to say, 'Do what I says!' To a child wearing a party hat, Martin suggested, 'Let's do party!' His contributions on this occasion surprised Mrs Clark, who thought them quite advanced 'for Martin'. In February, Mrs Clark was explaining to the children that when printing an upper case 'E', the 'perfectly correct way to make it' was to make the top and the bottom 'about the same size'. Martin interjected, with great interest, gesturing with his fingers, 'But, not like this big one, and this one same size' – meaning, I think, that the middle horizontal line should be shorter than the other two. Mrs Clark was anxious to move to another activity, and it was not clear whether or not she understood Martin's contribution. She only minimally acknowledged it and then began giving children instructions for the next activity.

By the end of the school year, Mrs Clark was convinced that Martin was a fairly bright student who would probably require some adult-monitored structure so as to work to his potential. Mrs Clark did not regard his English language abilities as an impediment to his learning and she did not recommend testing for specialised ESL support in Grade 1. In her view, Martin was prepared for Grade 1 but his behaviour and 'flightiness' were a still-relevant potential concern.

Julie

Julie and her younger sister were born in Canada to Polish-speaking parents. Cousins, aunts and uncles lived nearby. Julie's mother had cared for her children, speaking Polish, since their birth. Julie had used English a little while playing with English-speaking children in the townhouse complex where she lived before starting school. She had also attended one year of an English-medium pre-school programme. Her mother thought that Julie started pre-school speaking Polish appropriately for her age but knowing only 'a few words [of English], not much'. By the time she began kindergarten, her mother noted that Julie spoke much more English and that she insisted on speaking English with her younger sister. Julie's mother told me in November that Julie was starting to speak quite a bit of English with neighbourhood children. She had noticed that Julie was forgetting some Polish vocabulary and that her pronunciation of Polish, especially difficult sounds, was beginning to sound like an English speaker's.

Dr Karwowska assessed Julie's Polish skills in February and in June. She noted in February that Julie was doing a great deal of code-switching to English while speaking Polish, mostly because her Polish vocabulary, especially in the school domain, was undeveloped (or dwindling). Dr Karwowska also documented productive syntactic restrictions in Julie's Polish as well as receptive difficulties caused by syntactic distinctions in Polish not made in English. After the June meeting, Dr Karwowska thought overall that Julie's Polish proficiency was limited and that 'she is losing Polish in a steady way'.

Many of my notes, and the audio- and video-tapes show that Julie was relatively quiet in her classroom and that she spent a good deal of her time watching other children, listening to them and watching her teacher. At the same time, I was also impressed by the extent to which Julie socialised with others in her classroom. She appeared to have a series of preferred playmates throughout the year, but she also interacted with many other children as well. Her preferred playmates in her morning kindergarten at the beginning of the year were Alice, an anglophone girl, and Oscar, a boy whose family spoke Laotian. Alice moved away from the school in December and Oscar also moved away in April. However, by about January, Julie had also become particularly friendly with Amy (one of the focal children) and Melanie, in whose home English was used. All year, in the afternoon class, Julie interacted preferentially with Agatha, her cousin. With Alice, Oscar, Amy and Melanie, Julie spoke English, of course, but with Agatha she initially almost always spoke Polish, with a great deal of code-switching between English and Polish. Later in the year, she and Agatha spoke more and more English with each other.

Julie's interactions with her playmates varied, and Julie and Alice's interactions frequently appeared somewhat competitive. Oscar often took quite a protective stance toward Julie. In November, I observed Julie and Oscar playing a Concentration game when Alice approached them and asked to play, which they allowed. Alice won the game and Julie exaggeratedly hung her head, communicating distress.

Oscar appeared worried about her, stroked her back, said several comforting things and asked Alice if Julie 'could go first' as the next set of cards were laid down. At the end of November, Alice and Julie were playing at the sand table together. I could not record their conversation, but my field notes say: 'Alice is being very bossy toward Julie, but Julie's taking it'. In early December, the two had the following conversation:

(30)

As they are doing a Christmas craft – gluing triangles to one another and then decorating the 'trees' with sparkles and crayons.

Alice:	*(To Julie)* You're copying me!
Julie:	No.
	(Pause 5 seconds)
	Where'd you get that? *(referring to some sparkly paper Alice has. Laughs.)*
Alice:	I can't tell you.
Julie:	Nice! *(showing me [KT] some shiny paper she has)*
	(laughs) I did it the wrong way!
Alice:	Don't copy!
Julie:	I'm just gonna . . . *(runs away to get more paper. Returns)*
	See! *(laughs)*
Alice:	It's not funny, Julie!
Julie:	Let's see. Guess where I'm gonna stick it. I'm making this for my mom. She was sick. She was having a <u>big</u> cough.
Surjeet:	*(comes to sit beside A and J. Speech does not appear connected with anything that has gone on so far)* And my sister said, 'LEAVE ME ALONE!' *(yelling)*
Alice:	Be quiet *(pause 3 seconds)* that's a big *(pause 4 seconds)*
	Oscar comes over and whispers to Julie.
	Hey, Julie, remember no secrets in this school? What did he tell you?
Julie:	He said /bey uw:::: læ læ/[13]
Alice:	It's gonna hurt my feelings.
Julie:	Okay, I'll go ask him.
	(She moves to Oscar – whispering) Can I please tell her? She's my best friend.
Alice:	I know what he said.
Julie:	Should I tell her? *(to Oscar)*
Alice:	I won't tell no one. *(to Oscar)*
	Oscar nods.
Julie:	*(As if quoting, this is the secret)* He's my friend and he likes me and he likes you.
Alice:	*(whispering to Oscar):* I'm making something for Santa.

Surjeet:	I heard that.
Alice:	What did I say?
Surjeet:	You're making something for Santa.
Alice:	No I'm not.
Surjeet:	You're lying.
Alice:	No I'm not.
	(Pause 10 seconds)
Julie:	Tell me what you said.

Alice then whispers her secret to Julie and Surjeet walks away.

Julie maintained 'face' in this conversation, despite Alice's initial desultory attempts to threaten it.[14] First Julie denied she was copying Alice (copying was a practice of some ambiguity to be discussed in more detail in Chapter 4). Next, Julie announced that she had 'made a mistake'; she laughed and ignored Alice's rebuttal that the mistake was 'not funny'. Oscar's whispering to her then put Julie in a more powerful position than Alice (as someone in the know). Alice asked to be let in on the secret. Julie very quickly acceded, while maintaining Oscar's right to decide whether or not she could let Alice in on the information. Julie did not acquiesce to Alice's initial attempts in this conversation to shame her, and Oscar's intervention allowed her to speak from a more powerful position than Alice for a turn or two. I did not notice whether Oscar had observed the girls' interaction before he moved in with his secret, so I do not know whether he intervened intentionally, to 'protect' Julie. However, he very effectively helped her resist the subordination Alice was trying to set up. Although Julie was not subordinated, Alice's attempt to subordinate Surjeet was presumably more successful.

Julie's interactions with Melanie appeared much less fraught with difficulties than those with Alice. The following conversation took place in mid-November:

(31)

Melanie and Julie playing with farm animals, moving them around, making fences around them. Talking about big and small cows.

Melanie:	See I can tell where they are.
Julie:	No the cows has to be here. Here's grass and there's grass too. This cow doesn't want to stay up. *(complaining)*
Melanie:	We've got some people coming to feed [the horses.
Julie:	[Here's a horsey.
	And the big horse. *(Plays with the big horse.)*
	(In someone else's voice) 'Remember I have to get on the horse.'
Melanie:	Do you?
Julie:	This horse doesn't want to stand! *(irritated, her own voice)*
Melanie:	Some do, some don't.
Julie:	This is their horse – here's one cow.

Melanie:	You tell me which dog you want to use?
Julie:	No. I like this one.
Melanie:	How about we use two?
Julie:	I like this horse.
Melanie:	Me too, I'll put dog the fence
Julie:	**** I have to go to the washroom.

This play with Melanie appeared relaxed and enjoyable. Julie entered into storying play (*'Remember I have to get on the horse'*) at one point and the two negotiated how they would handle both liking the same horse. Speaking with someone else's voice occurred in some of the children's storying play, especially in the housekeeping centre, but some children never engaged in it.

In numerous examples, Julie was able to deflect criticism and/or to maintain a desirable position within her classroom. Once in November when children were cutting out pictures of 'foods bears like to eat', she initiated a subordinating sequence about Harvey:

(32)

Julie:	Does Harvey eat garbage?
	Children laugh.
Alice:	Does Harvey eat a roof?
Julie:	Does Harvey eat a roof?
Earl:	*(putting scissors in mouth)* Does Harvey do this?
	Children laugh uproariously.

Later I recorded:

(33)

Wesley:	Julie's a fish!
Julie:	And you're a bear!
Wesley:	Gr: ow: l::
	Julie smiles.

Here, Julie deflected Wesley's potentially subordinating game with her.

On many other occasions, Julie was able to resist or deflect others' attempts to dominate her, for example:

(34)

Julie goes to computer. Tries to figure out where to turn it on. Ryan notices and comes over and does it for her (!) She looks at the screen and does nothing. Oscar comes over and points to the alphabet across the top. Alice comes over and grabs Oscar's hand off screen.

Alice:	Can I play next?
Julie:	No.
	Julie singing A-B-C song and kind of randomly pressing buttons. Oscar is trying to show her non-verbally what to do.
Oscar:	My turn, Julie. *(Tries to wiggle onto the chair.)*
Julie:	Wait.
	He gets off the chair. She clicks on another 'game'.
Julie:	*(pointing at an icon, to me)*: Is this a /hɔrz/?
Oscar:	A *horse*! It's not a /hɔrz/!
KT:	Oh, a horse. No I don't think so.
Julie:	It IS a /hɔrz/.
	Harvey joins the group of kids around her. Also Ryan who pushes some keys. Ryan starts a new game. Julie is still on the chair.
Julie:	Don't push.
Harvey:	Julie, it's my turn.
Ryan:	Harvey, go wipe your nose.

Julie looks at me (KT) and grimaces. Harvey goes away, she leaves.

Julie was able to maintain her position, even though she was neither very expert at nor very interested in the computer over which the children disputed. She also contradicted one of my statements and continued her play without pause.

The afternoon kindergarten included not only Julie's cousin Agatha but also several other Polish-speaking youngsters. Agatha spoke Polish well, but was also an experienced English speaker because of her pre-school attendance at an English-speaking daycare centre. In the afternoons, and on the playground, Julie played with Agatha a great deal. The girls increasingly played in English as the year wore on (speaking almost exclusively in English by about April, despite their teacher's lifting of the first language ban). Although Agatha was not enrolled in Julie's morning kindergarten, Julie's having this powerful part-time ally, with whom she had strong and long-standing ties outside the classroom (and school), may have been important in how others (including her teacher) came to see her in school.

Julie often attempted to involve adults in conversation and mostly succeeded. More than any of the other children, she would try to engage me in brief conversations, asking to look at my field notebook, asking to write her name in it and so on. She also made friendly overtures to the teacher aide who supervised the children while they ate their lunches and played outside at noon. When 'Mrs B' entered the classroom at lunch, Julie would run to her, mock-wailing in a high-pitched voice indicating, I think, extreme pleasure, 'Oh, Mrs B!' and hug her. Julie switched affiliations to a new aide after Mrs B moved to a new school; her behaviour with the new teacher aide was very similar. Both women accepted Julie's initiations with what looked like pleasure and Mrs B told me that she found Julie a 'sweet little girl'.

More than any of the other children, Julie asked others for help when she was unsure of a vocabulary item. Typical was this interaction in January:

(35)

Ryan:	Look at that wiggly, swiggley, miggley worm.
Julie:	What's a worm?
Ryan:	It's something that crawls in the grass! *(surprised)*

This interaction, in which Ryan provided a definition for her, showed Julie as seemingly unafraid that her display of 'not-knowing' would be a problem for her. As in her laughing proclamation in Excerpt 30, 'I did it the wrong way', Julie did not seem unduly concerned about her occasional inexpertise.

To an extent not noticed with respect to the other focal children, Julie discussed her first language often with other adults and children in her classroom and displayed her competence in Polish to others. Martin in her morning class, initiated several Polish conversations with her. She also spoke Polish with Agatha and some other Polish-speaking children in her afternoon class. One morning in February Julie tried to teach Cathy (an anglophone girl) and Oscar some Polish:

(36)

Julie goes to chart with pictures and English labels written by the pictures. Cathy and Oscar are eating their snacks at the adjacent table. Julie points to a picture of a bird.

Julie:	This in Polish means <u>ptak</u>.
Cathy:	*(points to a frog)* What does this say?
Julie:	Um::::. *(referring to a different picture)* <u>Jajeczko</u>. *(diminutive of egg)*
	Cathy points to bear.
Julie:	Misiu*(mispronunciation of Polish <u>misio</u>)*
Cathy:	What?
Julie:	Misiu.
Cathy:	Misiu.
Julie:	*(pointing to a picture of a Christmas tree).* <u>Hoyinka</u>.
Cathy:	*(to Oscar)* Do you know how to count in Polish?

Cathy and Oscar start talking about something else. Julie continues to look at the chart, saying: 'I know what this means . . . '

On other occasions as well, Julie explicitly discussed her and other children's knowledge of Polish. She appeared proud of knowing Polish and more than any of the others, she acknowledged her affiliation to her first language and considered that others might be possibly interested in it as well.

At the end of the year, Mrs Clark assessed Julie as having made good progress in linguistic as well as academic skills. She was confident that Julie would have a successful year in Grade 1 and probably would not require any further special assistance with English.

Harvey

Harvey was the oldest of three boys in a Chinese family. I initially thought (as did Mrs Clark) that Harvey spoke Chinese at home. He was enrolled in the afternoon Language Development class on the basis of that supposition. However, interviews with his mother made it evident that English was Harvey's first and only language (cf. Toohey, 1996). Harvey's mother reported that she and her husband, native speakers of Teochew (a Singaporean dialect of Chinese), had decided that they would speak to their children only in English so as to ease their way in Canadian schools. In separate interviews at the beginning of the school year, Harvey's mother told both Mrs Clark and me that Harvey 'was a very bright boy' and that she was glad he was in school because she felt he needed more stimulation than she could provide at home. She cited the elaborate Lego constructions he had been making, his attention to stories and his efforts to read, as evidence of his cleverness. Harvey's mother's English phonology was similar to his; Mrs Clark's suggesting later in the year that Harvey's English pronunciation might have caused him problems at school surprised both her and her husband.

Harvey's interlocutors often did not understand his utterances, particularly when he took 'long turns', and he appeared very frustrated by this.[15] Their not understanding him seemed related to their positioning of him in the classroom. A typical example:

(37)

Harvey with a small group of other pupils. Harvey initially unhappy because one of the children moved the crayons at the table on which he is working and he is unable to reach them. In the context of a relatively long utterance which neither I nor the children (I think) understand, Harvey says: /swɛtš/ [meaning, I think, 'stretch'.]

Edward:	*(laughing, mocking)* Trash???
Harvey:	*(twice)* I didn't say <u>trash</u>, I said /swɛtš/ *(angry and frustrated).*
	The children laugh and move the crayons farther away from him. Unable to sustain my observer stance, I say – I think Harvey wants to reach the crayons. Harvey, can you say 'Can you pass the crayons, please?' *He does, they do and then he leaves.*
Edward:	I don't like Harvey.

Harvey had many disputes with other children over resources; also other children frequently refused him access to play with them. Often, the other children appeared to ignore his verbal initiations. Once, for example, Harvey carried around a Bingo game and wanted playmates: he approached two other boys in the class (one anglophone, one Chinese-speaking):

(38)

Harvey:	Bingo, guys! *(enthusiastic)*
Earl:	Ah, stupid Bingo.

He asked another boy who did not respond and it was unclear whether the boy had not heard him, had not understood him or had just chosen not to respond. A few minutes later, Harvey said to me: 'Mrs Toohey, nobody's playing with me Bingo. Nobody ever plays with me'. Indeed, he spent a great deal of time playing alone.

Harvey coughed, sneezed and had a runny nose on many occasions. In addition, he was somewhat less physically adept than many of the other children. On several occasions, other children angrily reprimanded him for touching them, if he had inadvertently leaned on another child in the circle or bumped into them in a line-up. I observed children wrinkling their noses in disgust after the teacher told Harvey to wipe his nose. Other children often told Harvey to move further away when he sat down beside them in the circle. Excerpt 32 (cited earlier) illustrates a 'shaming' of Harvey, an episode initiated by Julie:

(32)

Julie:	Does Harvey eat garbage?
	Children laugh.
Alice:	Does Harvey eat a roof?
Julie:	Does Harvey eat a roof?
Earl:	*(putting scissors in mouth)* Does Harvey do this?
	Children laugh uproariously.

Considering himself an expert with the wooden trains, Harvey at the beginning of the year quite loudly directed others about play with them. Harvey frequently disputed with other boys about the use of the trains and it appeared often that the other boys resisted Harvey's commands. Frequently, disputes also arose when Harvey took classroom materials (glue, scissors, and so on) from other children. At times, Harvey became very frustrated with his classmates and expressed his irritation loudly. Often, as he made to snatch something, he would declare, 'You have to share!'

Harvey frequently sought interactions with the teacher and other classroom adults at the beginning of the school year. He reported when he felt he had been unfairly treated by other children and he initiated conversations both with the teacher and myself on occasions when he had apparently been unable to engage children in interaction. He frequently bid for the teacher's attention during circle time in order to relate long, often somewhat incomprehensible (to her) stories. Despite his frequent exclusion from activities with other children, he actively participated in teacher-led activities: he often answered teacher questions in the circle, usually participated actively in choral work and indicated enthusiastic interest in the stories read to the group.

Despite the skills that Harvey's mother had pointed out, Harvey began the school year apparently unfamiliar with pencil and paper. Initially he also had difficulty writing his name, colouring and using scissors and glue. By the end of the year, he would finish the daily assigned crafts quickly and was frequently reminded both by other students and the teacher to put his name on his work, to tidy his materials and to return equipment to its storage. Mrs Clark told me several times she was less convinced of Harvey's intellectual gifts than his parents. Doing crafts and displaying familiarity and adeptness with school materials (glue, scissors, and so on) in 'the school way' are clearly part of the practices of kindergarten and Mrs Clark judged Harvey as less than skilled in these areas.

Harvey's behaviour changed somewhat about the beginning of February. At the end of January, Abe (whose family spoke Kurdish) joined the class. Abe appeared seriously bewildered by the kindergarten activities. For a time, Harvey mentored Abe's involvement in classroom routines. Harvey reminded Abe where to put his backpack, when to come to circle, when it was snack time and so on. The boys sat next to each other in the circle and engaged in play at activity time. Harvey 'read' to Abe at book-sharing time. This enjoyable interaction with Abe did not persist: at the beginning of March, I observed the boys having a heated resource dispute (both wanted the same toy car) and thereafter the pair very seldom interacted. My fieldnotes include five occasions after March on which Abe blamed Harvey for mishaps in the classroom (when the baby chicks' aquarium got jarred, when the teacher reprimanded a group of boys for pushing while in line and so on).

Harvey used a variety of strategies for soliciting playmates, playing, handling conflict and finding affiliations in the classroom over the course of the year. In March, Harvey entered and sustained for about 20 minutes an interaction with two Chinese-speaking boys (Earl and John) in the afternoon class. During his interaction with the two (who switched from Chinese to English when Harvey was clearly involved in the play), Harvey was careful to situate himself as a 'track fixer'; he continued to offer the cars to the other two boys as train 'players' throughout the interaction:

(41)

Earl and John are playing with the Brio (train). Harvey comes up.

Harvey: Can I play?
Earl: NO!

Harvey:	I know, I'm just helping you. The bridge is very hard to do. You need a block underneath. *(He gets a block and puts it underneath.)*
John:	No!
	Earl says nothing.
Harvey:	I'm very smart, do I, Earl? *(No response from Earl. Earl keeps assembling tracks.)*
	You can try this *(offers another piece)*
	Earl accepts. They both laugh as engine races downhill.
	Track breaks. Harvey immediately tries to fix it.
John:	*(to Harvey)* See this car?
Harvey:	This too swippers [?] here.
Earl:	It's easy to make this, right?
Harvey:	Here are your trains. *(to Earl)*
	Harvey sits back as other two boys play.
	John, your train!
	Harvey gets up and takes it to John, then takes it back to Earl.
	Earl, John didn't need it.
	Tension seems to have gone down. Earl and John playing, Harvey watching.
	John, everything is going down.
	Abe approaches.
Earl:	Hey, no way! Not you guys play, just Abe! *(Earl trying to get Abe in and the other two out, but the attempt was not apparently successful.)*
Harvey:	I'm really good at helping Earl and John, do I? . . . This is more stronger.
	Harvey offers a larger engine to Earl.
Earl:	I don't want this.
Harvey:	I can help you with this?
Earl:	No, stop.
Harvey:	Why?
Earl:	Because I want these *(the other pieces).*

Harvey appeared to have found a successful strategy for access to the train and the train play, maintaining himself as an acceptable peripheral participant. Situating himself as a fixer, and as not a full participant in the play, may have allowed him to stay without the other two boys becoming angry with him and invoking the 'two kids only' rule, or leaving themselves. In similar kinds of interactions afterwards, 'the helper role' allowed Harvey access to the materials he wished to use.

In contradiction to his prevalent difficulties, Harvey engaged in a particularly friendly interaction with Martin in March. For about a month around Valentine's Day, the girls in particular engaged in gift-giving: During activity time, one, two, or sometimes more girls would draw pictures or make things and then address them to one another. Upon their receipt, they would then elaborately thank one another with hugs and kisses. In March, Harvey gave Martin a drawing gift, framing the gift as an Easter present. The boys had a private friendly conversation about when Easter was, checking the wall calendar. Later in the circle time, Martin smiled and winked at Harvey in appreciation for the gift. The teacher reported to me in March that she had observed Harvey having a much better time in kindergarten as well, and attributed this to his taking Abe 'under his wing' and thus 'developing social skills he did not have at the beginning of the year'. He also found a relatively reliable playmate, Mark, who seemed as interested in the wooden trains as he was and who appeared to enjoy their joint activities.

Mrs Clark told me in March and then again in June that she was concerned that Harvey's academic skills seemed to be at a bit of a standstill. In assessing him for the spring report card in March, she had noticed that Harvey was unable or unwilling to give information he had been able to relate some weeks before. He was also participating less and less in the large group literacy activities. I also had the impression that Harvey was engaging in fewer and fewer 'long turns'; from about February, I did not hear him tell the long stories I heard so often at the beginning of the field-work. He participated less and less frequently in circle time activities and became generally less conspicuous than at the beginning of the year. In addition, beginning about the middle of April, Harvey left the classroom periodically for school-based 'speech therapy'.

Harvey's identity in his interactions with other children appeared problematic for him at times. He often seemed unable to participate happily in all the activities in which he would have liked to engage. Although he could sometimes sustain enjoyable interactions with peers, his access to peer interactions was sometimes conflictual. Harvey actively and enthusiastically participated in activities which included Mrs Clark, although he may have reduced the intensity of those interactions over the course of the year.

Amy

Amy came to Suburban City from Hong Kong the weekend before kindergarten began, to live with an aunt, uncle, infant cousin and her grandmother. Her Cantonese-speaking maternal grandmother had cared for her since infancy. Amy's father (who lived in Hong Kong and visited Amy, with Amy's mother, whenever possible) thought that she knew 'almost no English' upon her entry to school but that she knew Chinese reasonably well for her age. Amy had attended a pre-school programme in Hong Kong that had focused on school readiness activities and Amy began school in Canada evidently very experienced using paper and pencils, crayons, scissors and glue. Unlike Harvey, Amy was not stigmatised, but rather usually petted by the other children. Shorter than any other child in the class but more physically adept than many, Amy was a favourite with many of the other children from the beginning. Each time I observed, at least one of the girls, anglophone or bilingual, was in close contact with Amy, holding her hand, leaning on her in the circle. Amy returned her classmates' physical affection and hugged and kissed them.

Amy spoke no English upon her entry to school. Initially she spoke very little English to other children, or to anybody else either in conversation, or during the choral recitations of the circle.[16] In addition, she initially displayed little interest in the stories the teacher read to the students. However, her silence did not prohibit her participating in activities with other children. Indeed, the other children appeared to enjoy her presence: She smiled at others a lot, and laughed easily and quietly. She began school drawing, painting and using kindergarten tools maturely in comparison with many of the other children. Active in the girls' February and March gift-giving, she frequently received gifts from other children and her own attractively completed gifts were valued by their recipients. At the circle, many of the girls bid for Amy to sit next to them. Quiet and compliant, she was a legitimate peripheral participant in most of the children's activities; she was often invited and was rarely denied access if she requested it.

Comments made by a female student in the afternoon class in January may explain some of her classmates' perceptions. After I had asked Amy a question, to which she gave no reply, Agatha told me:

(42)

Agatha: She's a little girl. Nobody can take care of her at home. So that's why she comes to school. She can't stay by herself. So she could come here and we'd take care of her.

Despite her 'little' image and her initial reticence, Amy easily let others know what she needed or wanted. Using gestures and pointing, she got classmates, the teacher and me to give her any physical assistance she required. In December, for example, she told classmates at the circle 'Some here!' and they rapidly complied with her request for more room to sit down.

In November, Amy began to participate verbally in classroom routines, answering 'Good morning, Mrs C' at roll call, and participating in choral counting and other choral activities. Beginning about the end of November and continuing for about two months, Amy treated her interlocutors to word gifts: she would come up, say a word, smile and leave. On several occasions in January, as I watched Amy work on a craft or a drawing, unsolicited she would tell me the names of her classmates, the days of the week or something else the children had been practising in choral recitation. Beginning about February, Amy began to approach her teacher, her classmates and me with phrases and short sentences. In February, she asked me to cut something out for her, saying: 'You get it out, this one here?' She began to participate in storying play with some of the other bilingual children in her class; primarily in the housekeeping corner, she participated in assigning roles and rudimentary planning. In the following conversation, Amy's minimal verbalisations were nevertheless sufficient to keep her part of the story line:

(43)

In the housekeeping corner. Julie and Amy are playing. Oscar comes over.

Julie: We are the sisters and pretend the mom and the dad died
             (Pause 4 seconds)
Amy: Yeah
             (Pause 3 seconds)
Oscar: Where's the dad?
Julie: That's okay, we're just pretending the dad died.
Oscar: And the mom?
Amy: Yeah
Oscar: Who's the mom?
Amy: *(gestures to Julie)* Her
Oscar: Oh.
             Oscar moves into the house. Amy is apparently not entirely happy to have him there. He starts to move things.
Amy: No!
             Oscar persists. She puts roof on the house and kneels on his finger.
Oscar: Oh!!
Amy: Oh, sorry. See!
Oscar: Why'd the baby fall down, Julie?
Julie: The mom and the dad died, but we're going outside. That's not the momma.
Amy: We're going to the kitchen to eat?
Oscar: Are you going to the beach?
Amy: No!
Julie: Hello, let's feed our babies.
Amy: Hello baby, let's eat.
Julie: Where is the died dad?
Oscar: I could be.
Julie: Okay.

As the year wore on, Amy's vocalisations in storying play and in conversation became more complex, but her interlocutors' help continued to be crucial in her communicative success.[17] A conversation in April, again involving Amy, Julie, Oscar and myself, illustrates this well:

(44)

Julie clutching her stomach, groaning and putting her head down.

Julie:	OUCHY! I think I'm going to die from this stomach.
Oscar:	You can't die in school.
Julie:	I think I'm going to die up to Hong Kong.
KT:	I don't know what that means.
Julie:	*(to Amy)* Do your mom and dad live in Hong Kong?
Amy:	Yeah.
Julie:	Do you live by yourself?
Amy:	Yeah, my grandma and my sister and my uncle. I lost my uncle. My auntie baby. Very bad.
Julie:	What's wrong with the baby?
Amy:	At night he WA WA WA
Julie:	Oh! Cry!
Amy:	My grandma have ouch her teeth. *(I think she is tying back to Julie's stomach pain.)*

Not only the children collaborated with Amy as she attempted longer turns. In May, Amy had this conversation with her teacher:

(45)

Amy:	Mrs C, at my house I saw a *(she runs over and points to a picture of a ladybug)* and my grandma *(Pause 5 seconds)*
Mrs C:	And she put him out? *Amy nods and smiles.*

Amy seemed more typically present at some activities than at others. I never observed her (or any of the other bilingual girls) playing with the anglophone boys, although some anglophone girls played with them. She seldom participated when the anglophone girls were engaging in storying play. However, at the beginning of March, she approached two anglophone girls who were playing with dolls and making stories. She asked, 'I can play here?' One of the girls said no, the other said yes and a discussion ensued between the two about whether three children at once were allowed to play with the dolls. They solicited the teacher's judgement and she encouraged them to restate the classroom rule for themselves. Amy then left.

Amy frequently initiated and engaged in conversations with Earl, the other Cantonese-speaker in her morning kindergarten class, and with him and John, another Cantonese-speaker in the afternoon class. In these Cantonese conversations (taped in the kindergarten and translated by research assistant Sarah Yip), she was forthright and assertive, as in this Cantonese exchange with John:

(46)

Amy:	I'm not going to play with you anymore. Your mouth smells.
John:	Yours too.

Amy: How many days are there to **hot dog day**? *[bold print spoken in English]*

John: Don't know.

Amy: You don't know, you say. If you don't tell *(discovers John has left the table so shouts to him)* If you don't tell, I'll squash you flat!

Sarah began during the kindergarten year to have periodic Cantonese conversations with Amy in her home. In 1994, Sarah described her impression of Amy as a bright, forthright, linguistically talented girl; she and another Chinese-speaking graduate student assistant were impressed with the maturity of Amy's Chinese constructions. The Chinese-speaking boys in her kindergarten appeared to defer to her during Chinese conversations and she could successfully direct their activities. In a play period with cars and trucks with Earl, for example, Amy constructed a story with characters around the play equipment and told Earl specifically what to do. Earl, often a play director in English, did as she told him.

At the end of the year, Mrs Clark was satisfied with Amy's progress. She hoped that Amy would not forget all the English she had learned while she was in Hong Kong over the summer visiting her parents. Mrs Clark was hopeful about Amy's preparation for Grade 1, believing that she would require some further help with learning English, but that she was quite a capable student.

CODA

In this chapter, I have described in detail the six focal children and interactions in the kindergarten classroom that seemed to be involved in the construction of their school identities. I have told stories which might be assumed to reveal 'who these children are' and whom they seemed to become over the course of the kindergarten year. In Chapter 3, I will discuss how each of these focal children was characterised in reference to the ranking practices of schooling. The information and stories given here will provide evidence for the nature of school identities and for what is obscured in the creation of these identities.

Notes

1.   This referral in fact never occurred since Randy's silence 'broke' soon afterwards. Mrs Clark did not inform Randy's parents that she was thinking about a possible referral for him.

2.   Wood *et al.* (1976) first offered the concept of 'scaffolding': when a more experienced participant performs those portions of a task beyond the competence of a less experienced participant, so that the latter can focus on those parts of the task she can perform. A great deal of debate has subsequently ensued about the use of this term. I here use it somewhat casually to mean one person helping another so that a particular task might be accomplished.

3.   The transcription notation uses the following symbols. Square brackets denote the onset of simultaneous and/or overlapping utterances. For example:

Randy: Who's   [been
Mrs Clark: [sitting in my chair?

One or more colons represent an extension of the sound it follows (e.g. Who::s).

Underlining indicates emphasis.

Asterixes indicate incomprehensible words.

Capital letters indicate loudness.

Pauses and details of the conversational scene or various characterizations of the talk are indicated by italics.

Pauses of more than minimal length were timed to the nearest second and are indicated in italics.

Phonemic transcriptions are indicated by slashes (/swɛtš/).

This transcription notation system is similar to that described in Ochs (1996).

4. The children had been taught and had repeatedly chanted a similar poem about 'Fall'.

5. In another conversation I had with some older children and their teacher in this school, they said their teacher had told them not to use their first languages. This teacher firmly denied having said this, having the strong conviction of the importance of first language maintenance, and she and the children had a heated discussion about whether or not she had uttered this prohibition. The discussion ended with one child saying, 'Well, maybe it wasn't you [who uttered the prohibition], but we thought that was what you thought.' What teachers say and what children hear may not always be congruent.

6. Dagenais and Berron (1998) discuss complexities in the home language uses of several families of Southeast Asian origin in Suburban City. Romaine (1995) discusses the 'normal everyday' phenomenon of code-switching in the language of most bilinguals. Many Canadian speakers of Punjabi use many English words throughout their Punjabi speech, and the transcripts of conversations in Surjeet's home with Punjabi-speaking research assistants displays this hybridity. Thus, though her mother sees her as primarily an English speaker, Surjeet has grown up in a bilingual home, with complex language practices that utilize the resources of at least two distinct language repertoires.

7. Though I did observe on the playground occasionally, I did not do it regularly; observation there was difficult because the playground was large and the children moved quickly among large numbers of others. I noticed Surjeet playing with older girls at recess sometimes, girls who appeared Punjabi in appearance. If she spoke Punjabi in interaction with those older girls, I did not hear it, but my observation was too incomplete for me to have strong confidence that she did not speak Punjabi.

8. In October, Surjeet brought candies to give the other children to celebrate her 5th birthday. My fieldnotes reflect my indecision about her behaviour on that occasion: Surjeet rubbing her eyes as she takes candy around the circle. Body very tight and turned away from other children. Looks like very stereotypical display of 'shy'. Is it?

9. On one occasion when I was watching a group of children in the classroom and not taking any fieldnotes, Surjeet came up to me, pointed to my notebook and said: 'You write, not just looking!' (she moves her hand as if writing).

10. Melanie appeared to direct activities in this conversation; she told Surjeet what to do several times during this interaction. However, she did ask Surjeet how to make bubbles and the emotional tone of their play appeared to me quite friendly.

11. This was the case possibly because the other girls were aware that Mrs Clark did not welcome tattling initiations.

12. Later that day, it seemed that Surjeet <u>had</u> made a phone: when she demonstrated the construction at a circle time, when Mrs Clark invited her to do so, she said it was a phone.

13. On several occasions I observed Oscar come up to children and whisper 'Ooo la la!' in their ears, whereupon both would laugh. Julie tried here to deflect Alice's interest in the secret, but Alice did not accept this and continued to press for being let in.

14. Hall (1995: 214) cites Bakhtin (1981) when noting: 'Our every use of language, while serving to respond to and move an interaction along at any particular moment, also serves as a sociopolitical statement indicating our stance toward the particular interactive moment, our place in that interaction and our positioning toward the others involved.' Although this statement makes firm theoretical sense, the just-quoted interaction, I think, particularly clearly illustrates this point.

15. At the end of October, his classroom had a Halloween celebration with several parents coming in to help both kindergarten teachers manage the children at several project 'stations'. At one point, Harvey spoke at some length to one of the mothers; I heard only a few words. The mother said to him, 'You're not speaking English, are you?' Harvey then repeated his utterance, but the mother turned to help another child.

16. Amy's period of silence in English in the classroom is similar to that noticed by other researchers with non-English-speaking school beginners (Ervin-Tripp, 1974; Hakuta, 1974; Itoh & Hatch, 1978).

17. For example, in the housekeeping corner, Amy was often given the role of 'baby' and her verbal contributions then were usually took the form of cooing and crying.

CHAPTER 3

Constructing School Identities: Kindergarten Meta-stories

> From the commonsense point of view, we can separate the articulate from the inarticulate and wonder why respectively they are the way they are. From the sociocultural point of view, we can only wonder how full members of the culture can come together and arrange for each other to look differentially able. (McDermott, 1988: 41)

This chapter examines McDermott's question of how the focal children came to 'look differentially able'. They took up and were assigned identities as students; this community somehow arranged itself so as to have successful and unsuccessful members. As I argued in Chapter 1, many Western European institutions engage in the important practice of ranking its members, and in so doing they attach persons to individualities (Foucault, 1972). Schools participate, many have argued, in these activities. In this chapter I will illuminate some of the metrics upon which children in this study were judged in this regard, and discuss how rankings based on such metrics ignore and suppress certain kinds of knowledge, while emphasising others in constructing the children's identities. McDermott (1988) urged interrogating the practices that stratify communities: in the case at hand, asking not why some children are better than others at learning English, but rather how and to what end do we evaluate some children as successful (learning 'more') and others as unsuccessful (learning 'less').

BEING A CHILD/BECOMING A STUDENT

Kindergarten is pivotal in the lives of many children and families. Many children commonly participate in larger communities of practice than the family before they begin school (neighbourhood groups, religious organisations, daycare, playschools,

61

lessons and so on). In addition, physicians and others officially norm children's 'development' from birth on (and parents, caregivers, instructors and others unofficially judge and rank children as well). Nevertheless, compulsory kindergarten attendance marks a substantial shift in how children's behaviour, growth and development are assessed and compared with others. Although children come to kindergarten as kinds of children, very quickly they attain identities as kinds of students, legitimate peripheral participants in classroom communities.

Kindergarten teachers explicitly bear the obligation to rank children's development and especially, to identify outlier children, those whose development in any particular area is 'delayed'. (Delay is a particular interest; children whose performances are outliers in the opposite direction are not usually accorded such attention.) 'Early identification' is seen as the key to remediating possible deficits in children's development, to 'normalisation', in Foucault's (1972) terms. Identification means assigning identities to children as students. In addition, not only teachers but also peers and the children themselves engage in these classroom ranking practices. In this sense, ranking is work done by everyone in classrooms.

Educators customarily look for causes of school demeanor and educational achievement (especially with regard to young children) in children's pre-school socialisation, familial experiences and cultural backgrounds. From a sociocultural perspective, identities are seen as constructed and reconstructed in activities (practices) in which participants position themselves and are positioned by others. Children's pre-school experiences have effects, of course, on what happens to them and affects whom they become subsequently in other arenas. However, practices being dynamic and situated, identities evanesce in time and shift with respect to context. Kindergarten presents a new community of practice to children, a community in which the specific practices themselves might be causal. This being the case, research could usefully investigate how these practices serve these kindergarten children, particularly in regard to placing children in the range of identity positions classrooms offer.

ASPECTS OF SCHOOL IDENTITY

Foucault (1972, 1979) argued that positioning occurs through discourse enacted in particular institutions. This discourse provides metrics and hierarchies with which to compare and differentiate people on the basis of their relation to standards. In kindergarten, such judgements are made on several criteria so as to position children with regard to 'school discourse'.

This chapter analyzes the stories and information from Chapter 2 under the following headings, with the recognition that the distinctions are artificial and that these aspects of school identity are in reality closely interrelated. Of course, school identities are constructed on the basis of standing on a large variety of overlapping metrics; however, the following seemed most salient in the present case:

(1)   Academic competence.
(2)   Physical presentation/competence.
(3)   Behavioural competence.
(4)   Social competence.
(5)   Language proficiency.

Language proficiency, the aspect most frequently evaluated in traditional SLA research, here incorporates insights from the analyses of the other aspects.

Academic competence

Many researchers concern themselves with how schools apply definitions of academic competence to particular children. Work on assessment of academic knowledge and skills has long been a major focus of educational research, and some researchers have been concerned with issues of group performance on such assessments (cf. Luke, 1995). The evaluation practices of primary classrooms are relatively standard – teachers (as well as other children) observe individual children's performance on school tasks throughout the year, and teachers 'test' the performance of children on a set of (often government-mandated) tasks and procedures.

Of the six focal children in this study, by the end of the year Mrs Clark judged Amy, Martin, Julie, Randy and Harvey as academically 'average' and adequately prepared for Grade 1, at least as adequately prepared as other 'normal' students. Although she acknowledged 'great progress' in Surjeet's classroom performance, Mrs Clark was beginning to suspect that Surjeet had learning difficulties above and beyond her 'ESL-ness'; she recommended that the Grade 1 teacher have Surjeet assessed for possible learning disabilities. Later, on the basis of testing by one of the ESL specialist teachers and on Mrs Clark's recommendation, Amy and Surjeet received specialist ESL support in Grade 1. The other children were deemed to have 'enough English' to participate in classroom activities without specialist instruction.

My research did not aim at examining in detail the assessment practices in this classroom; hence, my observations with regard to assessment of the children's academic performances remain tentative. However, it is productive to consider variability in children's performances in particular classroom activities. Surjeet, for example, appeared most visibly to have academic 'problems' when Mrs Clark asked her to speak in front of the whole group of children or asked her questions during assessment sessions. She also sometimes appeared incoherent when speaking to other children, as evidenced by the dispute with Nina (Excerpt 17, Chapter 2). Surjeet's disorganised and incoherent verbal productions seemed to occur most often in conversations in which she perceived herself to be under threat. An observer who watched her listening to her classmates, participating in choral activities near the end of the year, playing 'Concentration' or delivering Valentines might have been impressed with her focus, memory and strategies for problem-solving.

However, her teacher and classmates found the competencies she displayed were not so visible as her problems. These problems might have been, at least to some extent, a result of her effort not to get caught 'not-knowing' or 'not-able' (cf. McDermott, 1993).

All speakers display verbal disorganisation and incoherence at times. Julie sometimes was observed 'not-knowing' in her classroom. She customarily checked vocabulary with other children and on several occasions she queried the meaning of a word (e.g. 'What's a worm?', Excerpt 35 in Chapter 2). McDermott (1993), in an analysis of how a diagnosis of 'learning disability' came to be applied to a child, suggested that in classrooms 'mistakes' are regarded sometimes as just mistakes, not potential threats to self. Possibly this notion explains Julie's apparent comfort with this practice. If not knowing the meaning of 'worm', for example, was for her no particular threat and she had no need to hide her incompetence in this regard, she could engage in a practice (checking) that Wells (1986) suggested as particularly facilitative for keeping conversations going. Some of the other children, on the other hand, might have seen the potential costs of checking vocabulary too great to risk.

Randy, for example, never visibly checked vocabulary with other students, but the verbal scaffolding Mrs Clark and some of his classmates provided for him may have served much the same function. Randy's participation in the choral activities of the circle was also 'scaffolded'. By having access to the linguistic resources of his teacher and some of his classmates, Randy could participate, though initially very minimally, in classroom activities. Thus, he had enough time to practice and appropriate the language he needed to participate.

The most salient events in the construction of Martin's school identity concerned his compliance with directives (to be discussed below in the section on behavioural competence). However, with regard to academic competence, Martin's occasional competent and thoughtful verbal responses did not seem as salient in how Mrs Clark and his peers perceived him as his also-occasional confused responses did. Classroom practices that elicit thoughtful speech from children may not necessarily be those on which the judgements of academic competence most rely (see Chapter 5).

Harvey presented other complexities with regard to ascription of academic competence. Though his mother believed (and told Mrs Clark and me) that he was a 'very bright boy', Mrs Clark was not so convinced. She cited to me Harvey's incompetence with printing, using scissors and other mediating means of the kindergarten. By the end of the year, Mrs Clark judged Harvey to have 'speech pathologies', but she felt he would have little difficulty with the Grade 1 curriculum.

Before beginning school, Amy had little or no experience speaking English. However, she came into kindergarten already familiar with the use of many kindergarten materials and keenly interested in completing the craft projects the teacher set up every day. She gradually over the course of the year came to participate more and more actively in the conversations the classroom offered, in particular ways (often, as has already been discussed, as a 'petted baby'). Mrs Clark's judgement that Amy was of average intelligence, and would be only temporarily handicapped by her lack of experience with English, no doubt rested on Amy's increasing participation in classroom conversations, as well as her adept participation in the classroom craft activities. This ascription of academic competence to her did appear related to aspects of Amy's physical presentation and movement.

Physical presentation/competence

Aspects of the children's physical presentation include matters such as their size relative to other children in the class or their colouring, as well as their physical agility and competence. Amy, for example, was smaller than any of the other children in her class, and smaller than any of the children in the other kindergarten class. Children clearly noticed this; indeed Agatha commented, 'She's a little girl' and told me the school was providing a kind of daycare for Amy. Sometimes children tied Amy's shoes for her or lifted her up as they might a much younger child. On the other hand, they also noticed and admired her agility and prowess in printing, colouring and using scissors (perhaps more than they would have were she larger).

Many aspects of the children's physical presentation in the classroom seemed to be involved in their school identities. Their 'racial' characteristics might have been relevant; no one explicitly mentioned this (although in Grade 1, there was explicit evidence), but I do not think children were unaware of these matters. The children noticed and remarked upon Harvey's frequently stuffed nose. Hairstyles, haircuts and clothing were also sometimes matters for comment, both by the teacher and from other children.

In addition to presentation, the teacher and other children noticed and commented upon one another's movements in the room and upon their familiarity and experience with kindergarten tools (glue, scissors, crayons, etc.) and particular ways of using these tools. These observations are part of how identities were built up; recall the conversation about Harvey's scribbling (Excerpt 18 in Chapter 2). Children noticed other children's ways of moving and of manipulating balls, hoops and other mediating means of their playground play or their physical education curriculum. And Mrs Clark, of course, evaluated children's physical development as well as their academic development.

Some of the children (Julie, for example) seemed able to maintain a place for themselves in their classroom, while for others (like Surjeet) that position seemed much more precarious. Comparing Julie's and Surjeet's reactions to requests or commands to yield their position on chairs at various times in the classroom (cf. Excerpts 19 and 34) makes clear the connection between physical presence, status and identity. Julie claimed space and time in her classroom, and her claim seemed legitimated by her peers. Surjeet, on the other hand, seemed much less legitimated in her claims to space and her bearing and gestures were not self-assured or expansive.

Classroom communities become interactive sites for about 10 months during which participants develop historically situated identities. Sometimes 'display' or physical presentation and physical participation in community activities become matters for verbalisation, thus reinforcing the notion of linguistic construction of identity. However, any individual's display and participation also become part of the community's shared historical knowledge, which may or may not be linguistically signalled or framed. Identities therefore develop not only 'in the moment' through discursive practices, but also through memory, which may or may not be framed in terms of language. Rogoff *et al.* (1993) warned that the focus on discursive practices in learning and teaching in Western cultures may not adequately describe matters in some non-Western communities. It may also be that Western observers have not adequately addressed physicality in considering human interactions. For second language learning research, it may be important to remember that learners have bodies as well as mouths, ears and brains.

Behavioural competence

One thread in educational sociology has for a long time analyzed the conventions and constraints on the behaviour of children in schools (e.g. Fine, 1985; Waller, 1961). This section deals with relations between the children and their teacher, specifically with regard to children's compliance with the teacher's directives (either explicitly or implicitly articulated) or other children's repetitions of them ('ventriloquations').

Kindergarten presents children with a more or less unfamiliar social milieu: many children, one adult, mandated activities. Some children may have had previous experience with such arrangements in daycare, pre-school or religious schooling, but some have not. Kindergarten teachers, aware that school practices may be unfamiliar to children, take pains to familiarise children with those routines and conventions as quickly as possible. They judge some children as more and some as less 'mature' in their acquiescence to the conventions.[1]

The kindergarten curriculum has many aims, but part of teachers' work at this level is to initiate children into school conventions, for example, silence upon adult command, expeditious movement through transitions, 'appropriate' body demeanour, adept use of the tools (scissors, paste and others). The selection of these skills is arbitrary (as are judgements of their performance; e.g. what is 'appropriate', 'adept' etc.). Mrs Clark usually judged the demeanor of all the girls in the focal group (and Randy) as appropriate. All these children appeared quiet on demand, their speech volume was customarily low, and all appeared experienced in the use of classroom resources.

On the other hand, Martin's and Harvey's[2] demeanours were problematic. Martin acquired very early in the year an identity as a 'behaviour problem' in some situations, from Mrs Clark's point of view, and she spoke to his parents about this. Some of his classmates also seemed to feel that Martin's behaviour often needed correction and they directed him frequently. One child's report that 'Martin talks rude', again provided evidence that ranking was done by the children as well as by adults. I did not directly question Martin about his perceptions of this matter, and so I do not know whether he accepted or resisted the construction of him as someone needing correction. However, at times he made strenuous efforts to be a 'good' school boy and to participate actively in activities organised by the teacher. Mrs Clark noted in his final report that 'his enthusiasm for our classroom activities has been an asset to our class'. When he obviously resisted Mrs Clark's directives, she framed this as his not 'paying attention'.

Martin and Surjeet were both judged as children who sometimes did not pay attention. Teachers and textbooks of pedagogy often define listening or 'paying attention' as a skill that needs to be taught. Schools also commonly use the notion of listening as obedience. Children who listen (or, often, those who do not listen) are sometimes described in fairly moralistic terms. Rarely do educators consider that children decide to listen or not on the basis of rational estimations regarding whether the material to be listened to has relevance to them.

Mrs Clark seemed less concerned about the girls' acquiescence to classroom rules than about the boys'. Surjeet had cried and clung to her mother at the beginning of kindergarten; Mrs Clark had worried that this behaviour would continue throughout the year and she was relieved when it stopped about two weeks after school began. After this, neither discussions about the girls, nor fieldnotes, nor their report cards ever mentioned behavioural difficulties. Like many schoolgirls, they were seen by their teacher and their community as 'behaving' appropriately. Neither Mrs Clark nor most of the other children understood Amy's occasional relatively aggressive statements in Cantonese to her interlocutors and thus, could not use them in making judgements about her behaviour. Mrs Clark read translated transcripts of Amy's Chinese interactions after the year was over and was surprised by them.

Randy began school as a silent participant; his silence in his classroom became a matter of concern to Mrs Clark in November. She was about to refer him for psychological testing to one of the district psychologists, but before that occurred, Randy 'broke' his silence and began to say some few things to Mrs Clark and later to the other children. His classroom demeanour as frequently quite silent was thereafter not a problem in Mrs Clark's opinion and she was delighted with the 'progress' she felt he had made over the course of the year. In fact, she used his quiet participation in classroom events as evidence of his maturity and readiness for Grade 1.

Social competence

Social relations with other children are another way in which judgements about children's behavioural competence are made. Many researchers have investigated how children interact with one another in classrooms and schools. I therefore searched my data for examples of the focal children's social relations with other children to speculate about how they are assigned and assign themselves, particular positions with peers.

Harvey apparently had the most disputes with other children especially early in the school year, and was sometimes excluded from play. Children mocked him and gossiped about him. His position with peers was rarely powerful or comfortable. Mrs Clark understood Harvey's difficulties to result from his personality, his phonology and his physical characteristics. The accommodations he made over the year to his classmates' demands (often becoming a 'fixer', less fully participating in the play) lessened the number and intensity of disputes in which he was involved. Mrs Clark defined these accommodations as the 'acquisition of social skills'. Contrary readings could point to difficulties in interaction as resulting not only from Harvey's actions in the classroom, but also from the classroom group itself. Clearly, the 'social skills' Harvey required to participate in play with others were different from the social skills other children, differently positioned, employed.

As the year wore on Surjeet began to have more apparently problematic interactions with classmates. Frequently subordinately positioned, she did not always appear able to contest that subordination, and her attempts to counter the subordinating efforts of other children rarely succeeded. In fact, the focal children were less often able to contest their subordination than might have been expected or desirable. At the beginning of the year, Harvey attempted to resist subordination loudly and fluently, but by the end of the year, his resistance seemed subdued. Martin frequently stopped doing something when told to stop by other children. He was thus positioned as subordinate, as someone who did not know what to do or who was doing the 'wrong thing'. When he told a child holding, in his opinion, too many cupcake holders, 'It's not to behave some lots', (Excerpt 28, in Chapter 2), it was apparent that the other child did not understand his reproach and continued to maintain her hold on the cupcake holders. Amy, when told to be the baby in 'housekeeping' play, often did play the baby; on the one occasion I observed when she claimed 'mother' position, Julie, her playmate said, 'We're both the moms'.

Amy's position as a 'cute little girl' in her classroom is instructive of the range of identity positions available in her community. Although obvious rewards accrued to someone who was pleasant, compliant, small and non-assertive, Amy occasionally 'acted from' a more powerful and assertive identity position in her interactions with Cantonese-speaking boys. At this point in her learning of English, this voice of forthright assertiveness only became apparent in her Cantonese interactions. There were, of course, costs associated with the identity position Amy occupied with English classmates. The possibility of her limitation to 'repressively stereotypic norms of gender appropriateness' (Bryson and de Castell, 1997: 98) was always there. Amy's compliance with being constructed as a 'cute little girl' (an identity highly unstable in its rewards) did not appear to help her claim a powerful position in her kindergarten.

Randy and Julie appeared to be the only children in the focal group who success-fully resisted other children's attempts to subordinate them. They used different methods: Randy typically ignored subordination moves and hence did not receive many; Julie resisted through engaging in counter-discourse and by making affilia-tions with other children who would come to her aid when subordination loomed.

Children's social relations in this classroom were not, of course, all disputatious. Children often acted out friendly relations with one another and the classroom predominantly created the impression of an extraordinarily peaceful and harmo-nious place. The language required to express friendship and care appeared easily accessible to the children. They heard a great deal of this kind of speech from Mrs Clark, who, for example, almost always referred to the children as 'friends'. While the language of 'friends' may be easily available, probably not much school curric-ulum focuses on how to address issues of power and conflict in the classrooms of young children, but the observations made here suggest these issues require atten-tion.[3]

Language proficiency

Being 'ESL' was an ascribed aspect of the identity of each of the focal children at the beginning of their kindergarten year, but it was a label from which some of them, in some sense, graduated. Despite the sometimes ingenious ways that the children had found to participate in classroom activities (e.g. Amy's taking on 'baby' roles in storying play; Randy's enthusiastic participation in 'circle' activities; Surjeet's careful attention to the activities of her peers), part of the teacher's legally defined responsibility was to evaluate some children as having 'not enough English' to participate, without specialist teacher support, in classroom activities.

Mrs Clark made her initial identification of the children as 'ESL' on the basis of interviews with the children and their parents before school began. At these inter-views, she asked children's parents who had indicated on the school entrance form that a language other than English was used in their homes, whether they wished their children to attend the afternoon Language Development class after 'regular' morning kindergarten. The children thus enrolled in the Language Development class were defined as 'ESL' for purposes of identification in the school and also for funding arrangements involving the school district and the provincial Ministry of Education. At the end of the year, one of the school's specialist ESL teachers, not previously known to the children, formally tested them in an approximately 10 minute session; the children were to produce their names, the alphabet and short answers to questions. On the basis of their performance in these sessions, the specialist assigned them an 'ESL level', which determined whether separate provin-cial funding would or would not be available to support their learning in Grade 1.

It became particularly evident near the end of the kindergarten year that 'ESLness', a shifting identity, varies with funding practices and schooling arrange-ments. In May, in a cost-cutting effort, the Suburban City's school board decided to discontinue 'integration' of beginning ESL students as of the next September and instead to set up 'reception' classes (classrooms composed entirely of ESL students) on the basis of teacher recommendations. Thus, some already enrolled students would be 'un-integrated' and 'received' in special classes. Mrs Clark was dismayed by this announcement and told me, 'I worked hard to get all these kids ready for Grade 1 and I don't want them to go into a reception class'. Asked which of the children she would recommend for such a class, she said, 'Just Amy and Surjeet'; however, she was concerned that such an arrangement might mean that some of the other children would not receive necessary assistance. Furthermore, she was not even sure she should recommend Amy and Surjeet because she doubted that a 'reception' class would meet their needs. In any event, many teachers, school district officials, the teachers' union and others resisted the school board initiative. Although a few new reception classes were set up in the district the following September, none were in Suburban School and all the focal children went on to a 'regular' Grade 1 class. However, this incident exemplified the power of adults far removed from classrooms to affect children's identities in those classrooms. Those identities are assigned on the basis of the 'power/knowledge' of the adults in the system.

By the end of the year, Mrs Clark and the ESL teacher specialist designated four of the focal children (Randy, Martin, Julie and Harvey) as having 'enough English' to not need specialist support in Grade 1; they defined Surjeet and Amy as requiring this support. How classroom social relations entered into how children were seen as language learners is complex. Consider the case of Julie, who 'graduated from ESL'. Was Julie's success because of her personality, her motivation and/or her strategies (as a traditional SLA account of her 'progress' might predict), or can one understand Julie's success in ways that take her social context more seriously into account?

Julie had relatively easy access to many classroom interactions and resources. She successfully established friendly relations with the adults in her classroom. She seemed able to play with or beside the children whom she sought as playmates. When other children made attempts to subordinate her (a common practice of this and many other play groups, cf. Goodwin, 1990), she appeared able to deflect them, often with the aid of child-allies. On several occasions (including Excerpt 30 in Chapter 2), Julie's responses to threats of subordination (with the aid of her ally, Oscar) evidently helped her to appear powerful, keep her place in the interaction and continue to have access to conversation with peers. Although Dr Karwowska saw her as a child who was 'steadily losing' Polish, Julie was the only focal child who explicitly declared affiliation at school with the minority language of her background and she sometimes used it as a way to interact with peers, as shown in Excerpt 36 in Chapter 2.

In the cases of all the focal children, linguistic expertise, inheritances, affiliations and repertoires were complex. Surjeet and Harvey presented particularly dramatic examples of the non-utility of the dichotomies 'bilingual/monolingual'. Both Surjeet's and Harvey's parents had decided to raise their children speaking English, believing that knowledge of English would give their children a schooling advantage. The school, on the other hand, defined these children as 'ESL' and that definition had consequences – in kindergarten they were enrolled in a full-day programme. In contrast to Julie, both children's access to valued community resources (like interactions with peers) were somewhat ambiguous. They appeared neither powerful nor comfortable using one of the mediating means (English) of their classroom, despite the fact that they had more experience using this tool in other milieux than some of the other children.

The contradictions in these cases were myriad. Julie, who entered kindergarten speaking (in her mother's words) 'only a few words' of English, graduated from ESL in kindergarten. Surjeet, who had spoken only English before school, was considered to be 'still-ESL' at the end of kindergarten. A traditional SLA perspective might have it that Julie came to kindergarten with different cognitive, personality, learning style and motivational strategies and traits from Surjeet and that she was able, therefore, to acquire more English during her time in kindergarten.

A sociocultural view of language learning encourages considering how learners find ways to come to voice, what struggles are involved for them as they appropriate new ways of speaking, how their interlocutors permit their appropriation of new ways of speaking, and what social practices structure their appropriation of voice. In her classroom, Julie was a relatively privileged speaker, who had child and adult allies and access to many classroom resources. Rather than seeing her as being highly motivated to learn English, or as having internal traits or facilitative habits which predisposed her to learning, it might make more sense to think of her as a child who 'graduated from ESL' because she had enough access to experienced members of her community of practice and to their mediating means to be able to appropriate those means.

Surjeet, on the other hand, by the end of the year appeared to have no particular allies in her classroom; on several occasions others usurped her place in conversations. Her access to classroom resources (including conversations with peers) never appeared secure, and her verbal contributions at such times seemed somewhat incoherent. The community of practice of the kindergarten made this context very different places for Surjeet and for Julie. If the practices of their community had been different, if the girls' access to its tools had been different, their identities as language learners might have been different. However, how they were seen in terms of their academic, physical, behavioural and social competence overlapped considerably with how they were seen as language learners. These aspects of their identities interacted in complex ways to construct them as differentially able.

Randy's case points out other aspects of how classroom assessments of language operate. Randy developed in his classroom an increasingly powerful identity, and an English 'voice' that allowed him access to many classroom activities. His teacher and his classmates afforded him scaffolding that kept his place in conversations. At the same time, Randy denied affiliation to Punjabi and to the competence in it his parents and the bilingual researcher believed he had. He also discouraged his parents from participation in Punjabi community activities. His identity as an increasingly more powerful school boy was accompanied by a denial of affiliation to Punjabi.

These children's affiliation to and expertise in the languages of their milieux need careful examination. Although the school identified them as 'ESL learners', the children's parents sometimes ascribed conflicting identities in this regard. The children themselves appeared to be negotiating their relationships with the languages of their milieux in a variety of ways. The community of practice in which they spent their days made differential positions available to different children; those positions had a great deal to do with what they had access to and thus with what they were able to learn.

DISCUSSION

Postmodern and sociocultural theorists have stressed the importance of exploring situated discursive practices in the construction of identities, rather than seeing identity as reflecting 'essential' aspects of human behaviour. Bakhtin argued that people become who they are through communication and the dialogue between voices constitutes context. McDermott (1993) showed the importance of investigating the discursive practices that occur in classroom communities that permit stratifying of participants' 'abilities', assigning the participants' particular identities with regard to these abilities. Second language learning research has suggested that 'identities and beliefs are co-constructed, negotiated and transformed on an ongoing basis by means of language' (Duff & Uchida, 1997: 452).

I have been struck in my work with these children by the extent to which one needs to employ a broad interpretation of 'language practices' or communication when arguing that identity constructs and is constructed by discursive practices. Goffman argued that the ethological notion of 'display' is helpful in understanding positions of actors in social settings. As he put it:

> Assume all of an individual's behaviour and appearance informs those who witness him, minimally telling them something about his social identity, about his mood, intent, and expectations, and about the state of his relations to them. In every culture a distinctive range of this indicative behavior and appearance becomes specialized so as to more routinely and perhaps more effectively perform this informing function. (Goffman, 1976: 1)

I think in this case, as probably in many others, aspects of the children's physical presentation were involved in the construction(s) of their identities, and hence in their place in the hierarchy of the classroom. The children's physicality became another kind of 'discourse' in their struggle for identity.

Bourdieu discussed how language use and the use of one's body are implicated in power relations:

> One's relationship to the social world and to one's proper place in it is never more clearly expressed than in the space and time one feels entitled to take from others, more precisely, in the space one claims with one's body in physical space, through a bearing and gestures that are self-assured or reserved, expansive or constricted ('presence' or 'insignificance') and with one's speech in time, through the interaction time one appropriates and the self-assured or aggressive, careless or unconscious way one appropriates it. (Bourdieu, 1984: 474)

The focal children's differentially successful claims to physical space and discursive time in their kindergarten classroom were also evident in the way they played there. Play has itself been subject to many of the same theoretical analyses as the other classroom phenomena discussed here, with some of the same philosophical debates.

Varga (1998) noted that the play behaviour of children has been studied since early in the 20th century, the predominant view being that there is a developmental hierarchy from least to most interactive play. This notion of a developmental hierarchy and the consequently derived norms for play, has led to the understanding that children's interactional experiences result from internal, individual attributes. Children who have apparent difficulties in interactions with peers, for example, appear from this perspective as being 'atypical in development' (Varga, 1998: 314).

In contrast, Maclean (1996), Matthews (1996), Varga (1998) and others analyzed children's play in its sociocultural contexts, seeing children as responding to the constraints and possibilities these contexts offer. Varga, for example, examined episodes in which pre-school children were having difficulties in interactions with peers, showing that alienation developed when specific children were stigmatised by others. Rather than seeing alienated play as a behavioural incapacity in the stigmatised children, Varga encouraged observers to consider the social relations of alienation in play. Maclean examined the participation of a child in playground disputes to see how identity positions were adopted and assigned to children. He shows the dynamism of positioning, that identity construction for school beginners involves 'initiative[s] with which children use the discourse resources of the social group to achieve their ends' (Maclean, 1996: 172).

The focal children's identities were constructed with regard to aspects of their academic, physical, behavioural, social and linguistic competence in their first year of school. Evidently these children were positioned in a variety of ways with regard to these aspects of school identity. Particular school practices served to make visible certain aspects of their presentation of themselves and to obscure others from view. Julie's, Randy's and Amy's identities were constructed so as to position these children in relatively desirable sites, although there were ambiguities in their constructions. They seemed able to interact with a variety of playmates, using a variety of resources; their behaviour was not problematic from their teacher's point of view; they were constructed as developing appropriate physical, academic and linguistic (English) competence. The situation for Surjeet, Martin and Harvey appeared potentially more ambivalent. For these children, interaction with peers seemed less comfortable than it was for the other three children. Surjeet, Martin and Harvey occupied more frequently subordinated positions. Their teacher was less confident of their 'normal' development of a variety of competencies.

Learners' identities have definite and observable effects on what they can do in classrooms, what kinds of positions as legitimate peripheral participants in class-rooms they can occupy, and, therefore, how much they can 'learn'. A central notion of Vygotsky's (cf. Berk & Winsler, 1995) was that children with disabili-ties were restricted not so much by their initial disability, as by isolation and restriction from participation in the activities of their communities. Some of the focal children seemed to be developing/being ascribed aspects of identities that might lead to their isolation, or to restricted and less powerful participation in their community. If Surjeet were continually subordinated by her peers, and excluded from, say, the imaginative play episodes that appear so facilitative of language learning, could she get enough practice to get better at using English in those prac-tices? If Harvey continued to be sidelined to a less central position in play activities, he would not appropriate the language of powerful, centrally located players. Similarly, if Amy continued to occupy 'baby' and 'cute little girl' identi-ties in English, more powerful voices might never become available to her. If Martin continued to be seen as someone who neither listened nor did the 'right thing', if these perceptions became power/knowledge in his community, his efforts to ask sophisticated questions and to do things creatively might be thwarted and unrecognised.

Certainly classroom evaluation practices reinforce our notions of identities as fixed and immutable. Teachers have the legal obligation to report to parents about what kinds of students their children are, and to assign ranks to those children on the basis of their evaluations. In some form or another, teachers need to report on most of the aspects of identity formation I have identified here. Thus, teachers are legally obligated to think in these ways about the children with whom they spend their time. Some teachers resent and resist the ways these evaluations shape their interactions with their students. Many teachers, at a variety of levels, believe that evaluations of this sort sabotage the community work in which their classes are engaged. Some teachers wish to think about their students as members of communities of learners. They recognise that the participants' differential skills and expertises are to be expected and that diversity is functional for the operation of the community (Rogoff, 1994). If 'not much fuss' were made about this differential expertise, except that full and powerful participation on the part of each member were to be encouraged, it might be that all members could learn. As Hall asserted:

> Active and frequent participation in the oral practices of one's group leads to the development of sociocultural competence and the ability to use the resources to display and/or modify this competence. (Hall, 1993: 143)

Careful examination of what 'active and frequent participation in the oral [and other] practices of one's group' leads to may be important. Taking the politics of communities into account may show what kind of 'development of sociocultural competence' is possible in particular milieux. Sociocultural competence in a community which ranks its members, might mean, for a frequently subordinated person, taking a less active and less powerful role in oral practices.

It may not, for example, be helpful to assert that learners are learning anything so unspecified as the 'target language' or even 'sociocultural competence'. Leung *et al.* (1997) and Rampton (1995) pointed out the complexities of children's social and linguistic identities in schools in England, showing the fallacy of assuming that minority language background children were, by definition, bilingual or were 'learning English as social and linguistic outsiders', in contrast with 'idealised native speakers of English' (Leung *et al.*, 1997: 546). Norton similarly pointed out:

> The central questions teachers need to ask are not, 'What is the learner's mother tongue?' and 'Is the learner a native speaker of Punjabi?' Rather the teacher should ask, 'What is the learner's linguistic repertoire? Is the learner's relationship to these languages based on expertise, inheritance, affiliation, or a combination?' (Norton, 1997b: 418)

It may be more accurate thus to recognise that learners of a language are participating in practices in which their particular subject positions become part of their interactive means. In this way, one recognises the politics of this situation – a situation in which participants struggle for positions in participation.

The traditional perspective on SLA explains 'facts' of learners' differential performance relatively unproblematically: because of greater cognitive ability, outgoingness, motivation, and other individually owned traits, some children acquire second languages more easily and rapidly. But there is a different perspective: that the community, in a sense, produces success and failure for the children. The identities available to these children with respect to ability were differential; different actions or practices provided the possibility for these identities to be assigned to and/or taken up by individuals.

Sociocultural theory has critiqued and reconceptualised assumptions of learning as individual internalisation of knowledge given by the outside world. McDermott (1993: 277), for example, argued that learning depends on the establishment of certain kinds of social relations that give participants enough practice in community activities to become 'good at what they do'. Conversely, other kinds of social relations can prevent participants from access to this amount of practice. In the case he examined, McDermott noted that in 'everyday life' and under the 'gentle circumstances' of having a friend work with him, a boy labelled by his school as learning disabled (LD), Adam, 'appeared in every way competent'. However, in classroom lessons and even more in testing sessions, Adam 'stood out from his peers not just by his dismal performance but by the wild guesswork he tried to do' (McDermott, 1993: 279), resulting in his characterisation as LD. McDermott argued that explaining the existence of these different Adams would be best accomplished by an approach that focused on:

> How much and on what grounds a person is liable to degradation in the different settings. What is at stake here in an appreciation of how much each setting organises the search for and location of differential performances and how much that search further organises the degradation of those found at the bottom of the pile. (McDermott, 1993: 286)

In some settings, Adam was preoccupied with not getting caught at – and other participants were preoccupied with catching him at – not knowing how to do something. In those settings, Adam was defined as LD. McDermott argued that learning in these kinds of settings centres around the potential for degradation. When he had limited possibilities to participate in whatever activities were ongoing, little time or attention available to get the information or little 'time on task' to become good at those activities, Adam acted LD. In other situations with little possibility for degradation (e.g. when a mistake could be dismissed as simply a mistake and not as a threat to self), Adam performed effectively.

McDermott asks with regard to Learning Disabilities (LD):

> Where is LD to be found? Is it to be found at all? Is it anything more than a way of talking about some children and available for analysis only as a kind of rhetoric? Might it not best be described as a political label, a resource for keeping people in their place, a 'display board' for the contradictions of our school system? (McDerrmott, 1993: 271)

He goes on to argue that although some children clearly learn differently or at different rates from other children, not all cultures make such a 'fuss over different ways of learning' as North Americans do (McDermott, 1993: 272). I have considered how six children labelled as learners of ESL construct and are assigned school identities. I have wondered throughout how it might be useful to consider 'being ESL' as McDermott considers LD: as a political label, a resource that has been used for keeping some students in their place. 'ESL identity' becomes a position, not an essence. Both Surjeet and Harvey were placed in an 'ESL' position analogous to McDermott's 'LD' position, both by teachers and by their peers.

Much SLA research has been concerned with assessing the different ways and rates by which learners seem to assimilate second languages. This traditional SLA research, and traditional classroom and school practices, 'make a fuss' over different ways and rates of acquisition. I have examined how six children in their first year of school began to be seen as participants in classroom activities, participants of a variety of sorts. As we have seen, classrooms are organised to provide occasions upon which some children look more and some less able, and judgements are made which become social facts about individual children.

McDermott noted that settings differ in their capacity to search for and locate differential performances, and that 'degradation is always a ceremony in which public agreement on what one can be degraded for is displayed and directed against the total identity of others' (McDermott, 1993: 286). The term 'degradation' may seem too strong in connection with kindergarten practices. North American teaching practices and the beliefs of the teachers of young children with which I am familiar, have a tact that would make identification of flawed academic performance as gentle and non-explicit as possible. Teachers intervene if they notice children roughly identifying flaws in the performance of others. In kindergarten, Mrs Clark was at pains to make sure that all her students experienced success and that they were all well prepared for Grade 1. The effects of our assessment practices are not really so gentle, however. This matter is taken up again in Chapter 6.

CONCLUSION

The focus in this chapter was primarily on how ranking practices operate within schools so as to position children differentially. Foucault's (1972) and Walkerdine's (1988, 1997) interest in how subjects are produced in practices provided background to my examination of schooling practices that produce different identities for children. At the same time that I wish to suggest the importance of the ranking practices of schools, I am heedful of Walkerdine's (1997: 63) reminder that 'a subject . . . produced in discursive practice . . . is not the same as an actual person'. Walkerdine argued for broad investigation of how persons take up or do not take up the discursive productions of them offered in their communities, arguing that sociocultural theory has not sufficiently theorised 'how subjects are produced in practices' (p. 59). In the same vein, Agre observed:

> To what extent should we view the children as putty that is being passively shaped into the discursive 'child', and to what extent should we view the children as active participants in the process? This is, to be sure, a point of instability in many theories of development . . . What is missing in each case is a substantive account of the children's noncooperation with the adults' plan for them. (Agre, 1997: 80–1)

The idea that persons internalise others' views about them is not new or specific to the theoretical perspective used here. I did not in this research investigate how or if the children whose ranking I discuss here took up the identities their school offered them, but I have provided information in Chapter 2 which contradicts the official story of who each child 'became' in the context of his/her classroom. Walkerdine (1988, 1997) provided observational data which explicitly contested teachers' and school's views of particular children. Interviewing subjects to ascertain their understandings of their own and others' views on these matters is another means of approaching this. I think such investigation is very important both for theorising about identity, but also so that educators might find ways to help learners sometimes resist the identities their institutions offer them. Eisenhart wonders:

> What leads an individual to pursue some identities and abandon or ignore others? It seems that we must find some way of understanding how individuals actively construct their personal goals, beliefs about themselves, and images of self *out of* the cultural models and socialisation processes to which they are exposed. (Eisenhart, 1995: 5)

Eisenhart shows how subjects in her study express narratives of self and how these stories might be useful as ways to understand how individuals take up and/or resist the identities offered them by their cultural context. The adults with whom she was working were easily able to express such self-narratives, and their different trajectories of learning within a new institution seem closely tied to their self-narratives.

Norton Peirce (1995) and McKay and Wong (1996) also underline the importance of investigating the dialectic between the identities offered to learners and the ways in which learners accept, resist or repudiate those identities. Again, their work was with older learners (adults and adolescents) who were able to report on their efforts in this regard. Finding ways to investigate how young children deal with this dialectic will be important future work. This matter is raised in greater detail in Chapter 6.

I do not suggest that the identities there children were assigned and/or established for themselves in kindergarten were maintained unchanging into subsequent grades. Rather, I argue here that identity is dynamic, that it is constructed in activity and that it is dependent on the power/knowledge of the adults (at least) in the system. Activities, in particular, change between kindergarten and Grade 1. The next chapter, which describes events in the Grade 1 classroom, focuses on classroom practices that regulate children's access not so much to desirable identity positions as to material, linguistic, social and other mediating resources.

Notes

1.   Because kindergarten teachers usually have little information about the children before they attend school (except, perhaps, in the case of younger siblings of children who have already completed kindergarten), many schools set up class lists on the basis of making sure that boys are not over-represented in any one class. This often rests on the assumption that girls are less resistant to adopting appropriate classroom demeanour than boys are, again on the assumption that girls on the whole are more 'mature' than boys on entry to kindergarten.
2.   Harvey's difficulties in his classroom more often had to do with disputes he had with other children (discussed in terms of 'social competence'), not with direct resistance to teacher directives, except the general tacit directive, 'get along with your peers'.

3.   Many of the classroom practices seemed explicitly organized to discourage disputes between children. The number of children participating with any one of the resource centres was set. When children covertly transgressed the quota rules, the level of disagreement in the activities seemed to rise immediately, and become loud enough for the teacher to notice and then enforce the classroom rule.

CHAPTER 4

'Break them up, take them away': Practices in the Grade 1 Classroom

---

> 'Neapolitans know a lot,' said Gianni. 'But they know it collectively. Break them up, take them away, and they're hopeless, just as stupid as anyone else. It's the city, the phenomenon of Naples itself, that knows something . . . ' (Hazzard, 1970: 38)

The Grade 1 classroom was located on the south side of the school next to the library; its windows looked out to a lane leading to the teachers' parking lot. This classroom was smaller than the kindergarten room and had fewer play materials. Randy, Julie, Surjeet, Martin, Amy and Harvey[1] were enrolled in this class along with 16 other children, four of whom were classified as ESL learners, together with Amy and Surjeet.[2] Ms Reynolds, their teacher, had taught for three years previously as a specialist ESL teacher. She had decided to teach a 'regular' class in 1995–96 and had been assigned this Grade 1 class.

Early observation in the Grade 1 classroom gave the impression that in some ways the community established in the kindergarten had 'broken up'. My initial sense was that the 'circle' of children who in kindergarten 'knew things collectively' (Hazzard, 1970: 38), was not so evident in Grade 1. Every year children and teachers do the social work of developing a new community. The Grade 1 class involved different participants from the kindergarten class: Some of the children were the same, but others had joined the class from other kindergarten classes, and some of the kindergarten children had been placed in other Grade 1 classrooms. In addition, the ESL specialist teacher withdrew Amy and Surjeet (and the four other children deemed to require ESL support) from the classroom several times a week for specialist instruction. I wondered whether their occasional absences meant that forming a classroom community would take more time. However, my sense that children in the Grade 1 classroom were becoming separated from one another increased as the year wore on. Finding ways to describe this separation motivated a shift in theoretical focus.

The kindergarten research had focused on practices which resulted in various constructions of the children's identities. Examining practices associated with their identity constructions over several grades might have provided interesting data showing the fluidity (and, perhaps, the fossilising) of school identities over time. However, I wished to shift focus from identity practices to community economic practices in order to investigate whether and how those were affecting the focal children's access to classroom language. I use the term practices in the sense of actions that are 'repeated, shared with others in a social group, and invested with normative expectations and with meanings and significances that go beyond the immediate goals of the action' (Miller & Goodnow, 1995: 7). The practices examined here are economic in the sense that they are concerned with the access of children to classroom resources. Lave and Wenger note:

> To become a full member of a community of practice requires access to a wide range of ongoing activity, old-timers, and other members of the community; and to information, resources and opportunities for participation. (Lave & Wenger, 1991: 100–1)

Here I wish to consider all these matters as resources and to examine how they were distributed in the classroom community.

None of the practices investigated here was in any way unusual in primary classrooms, although they differed somewhat from the practices in the children's kindergarten classroom. One difficulty in deconstructing routine, ordinary practices is that their everydayness renders them in some sense invisible. This does not reduce their importance; as Hall (1995: 209) noted, Bakhtin also urged attention to 'everyday, *ordinary* practices . . . as he claims that it is in our everyday world where life's most fundamental meanings are created'. Because everyday practices in the Grade 1 classroom differed from those in the kindergarten, and because a knee injury in November of the Grade 1 year constrained my movement about the classroom, I may have noticed more about where things were and how they moved. My own relatively brief difficulty with mobility underlined the recognition that where one can be and what one can do are importantly constitutive of what one can learn. The following describes some of the practices of the Grade 1 classroom which affected the focal children's communicative participation.

SITTING IN YOUR OWN DESK

Unlike the kindergarten, this classroom was furnished with individual desks and the children spent a great deal of time sitting at them. Figure 4.1 shows the placement

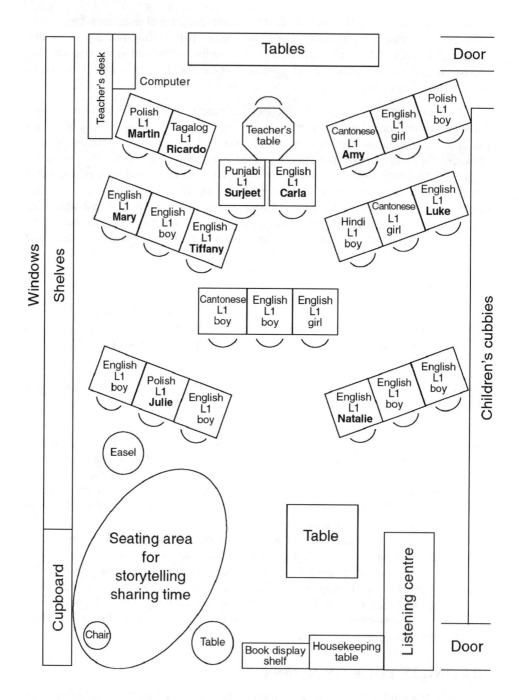

Figure 4.1 Seating arrangement in Grade 1 classroom

of furniture in the Grade 1 classroom and the seating arrangement of the focal and other children with regard to the languages used in their homes.[3] Although Ms Reynolds had enacted several other arrangements, this lasted the longest, prevailing from the end of February to the end of the school year in June. Figure 4.1 also shows the teacher's customary position; her position and the direction children faced establishes the 'front' of the room. Unlike in the kindergarten classroom where for each activity, children selected seating for themselves at tables (and where table groups changed often), the Grade 1 desk arrangements 'fixed' children's positions over long periods of time.

Commonly, teachers assign seating in classrooms to children on the basis of matters to do with management (e.g. they do not put two noisy friends beside one another, they put a noisy child beside a quiet one, they keep children who are unlikely to complete assignments or who might be suspected of daydreaming closer to the teacher's customary position). Ms Reynolds remarked that such considerations guided her decision-making in this Grade 1 classroom. As she received new information about children, as children joined or left the class or as she devised new strategies for encouraging them to complete tasks, she announced and enacted new seating arrangements. The children collaborated with the teacher in enforcing the classroom practice with regard to staying in one's own desk.

(1)

Luke: Can we work at somebody else's desks?
Ms Reynolds: No you work at your own desk. That's why you have one.

(2)

Surjeet goes over to Amy's desk.

John: Surjeet, get in your desk!

Many of the minority language background children in this classroom were seated near the front of the room and no children speaking the same home languages (other than English) were seated together.[4] Some of the anglophone children were seated beside and among the minority language background children; Ms Reynolds perceived these anglophone children not to be managing well the demands of the Grade 1 curriculum. With these children placed more closely to the position she usually occupied at the central hexagonal table, Ms Reynolds felt she could more easily help them. Evidently, she was able to monitor closely those children's conversations and actions. The anglophone children whom Ms Reynolds perceived to be clearly in no danger of difficulties in school were seated on the right at the back of the room. They occasionally engaged in lengthy conversations with one another, conversations which went mostly uninterrupted by the teacher. Natalie, for example, frequently read and described to her neighbours the plots of the chapter books she was reading.

Julie was seated in a back row; on either side of her were boys with whom she very seldom interacted. Ms Reynolds perceived Julie to have only minor problems with school despite her 'ESL' status, and to be well behaved. Indeed, Julie was very quiet in the classroom this year, although, as in kindergarten, she continued to be lively, socially active and verbal on the playground.

Martin was placed at the front corner of the room beside Ricardo, a student who had arrived in September from the Philippines and who was perceived to have the most serious English language deficiencies of all the children. Martin was so placed because Ms Reynolds felt that she could monitor his completion of tasks more effectively if he were closer to her. It was my impression that Martin spoke very little in his Grade 1 class and mainly to Ricardo, who sometimes had difficulty both understanding and responding to Martin's initiations.[5]

Surjeet was seated beside an anglophone girl who, although verbally active, seldom spoke with Surjeet. Surjeet interacted more with another anglophone girl seated across the aisle from her to her left (Tiffany), as well as with another anglophone girl seated in the same row on the far left (Mary). Surjeet's interactions with Tiffany were mostly friendly, but Mary frequently initiated unfriendly conversations with or about Surjeet.

(3)

Mary:	*(to Tiffany)* Don't go to Surjeet's birthday. It would be Indian smell *(wrinkling nose)*
Tiffany:	I won't.
Mary:	Will you come to my birthday? I'm Irish.
Tiffany:	OK.

Surjeet covers her ears and turns away.

Randy moved away in November. Before his move, he was seated at the back of the classroom between two anglophone boys with whom he had apparently enjoyable, sustained conversations. Ms Reynolds considered Randy one of her highest-achieving students.[6]

Amy was seated at the front of the room beside an anglophone girl who was frequently absent. Amy talked to this girl when she was present, and talked as well with the boy of Polish language background in her row. Her borrowing excursions (to be described later) afforded her more opportunities to talk to the children to whom she wished to talk.

None of the focal children was seated beside children with whom they typically chose to play at playtime. None of them was placed beside children from the same language background. By placing Martin, Amy and Surjeet close to her, Ms Reynolds could monitor and sometimes terminate conversations with the peers with whom these three did sit. Their seating facilitated conversations with her, but I did not see extended conversations of this sort occurring more often with these children than with others.

The children did not always sit at their desks. As they had in kindergarten, they also sat daily on the floor at the back of the room for the teacher's reading of stories, for discussions and for sharing time. Although Martin, Randy, and Julie were relatively immobile at such times, maintaining what looked like very close attention to the speaker, Amy and Surjeet were very mobile, with Surjeet often moving seven or eight times during a 10-minute reading. By the end of the year, both girls would start on the floor but move to their desks quite soon after the group had assembled itself on the floor, occupying themselves with tidying their desks, drawing or watching other children.

In kindergarten, Amy, Martin and Julie had sustained first language subcommunities within the larger kindergarten community. The different physical arrangements of the Grade 1 classroom may have contributed to the fact that, at least publicly within the classroom, the children very infrequently spoke their first languages except when they were addressed in them by their parents visiting the classroom at school opening or closing.

One of the objectives and apparent effects in placing the children in this way, then, was to restrict some children from conversations with some other children and for the teacher to watch some children more closely than others. On the other hand, the children would try to resist their physical separation from one another, to at least some extent.

USING YOUR OWN THINGS

The children in this classroom were individually responsible for keeping their resources for task completion (crayons, scissors, rulers, glue sticks, notebooks, and the like) in box-shelves built under their individual desks (unlike some other primary classrooms, in which resources are stored and utilised communally). Ms Reynolds frequently reminded children of the classroom rule to use their own materials, and some of the children, as well, reminded others.

(4)

Surjeet: Martin, use your own things, not other people's.

The children also engaged in a home reading programme in which everyday each child took home one of the school's collection of early literacy readers. These books were taken home in addition to those the children selected at the school library once a week.

(5)

Ms Reynolds: Boys and girls, it's silent reading. You each have to have your own book.

The under-desk shelves in which the children's materials were stored were short vertically, deep, dark, and placed so that children had to huddle low in their chairs, or get out of their chairs and squat on the floor to see inside. The children frequently lost or misplaced their individually owned materials in or outside their desks. In addition, when they lost or used up some or any of their supplies, the children were responsible for telling their parents to replace them. Many children's supplies were incomplete fairly soon after school opening. However, many of the children solved their problems with keeping and managing their own inventory of materials by asking other children to lend materials. Borrowing and lending led to social interaction, some conflict and physical movement in the class. Although some children most frequently borrowed from children sitting next to them, others would move to other children's locations to borrow. Ms Reynolds did not always tolerate this movement around the classroom and the children knew she could terminate their movements.

Julie's and Martin's lending and borrowing practices were somewhat simpler than Amy's and Surjeet's. Julie and Martin borrowed relatively infrequently and in no examples in the data was Julie asked to lend her materials to others. Martin borrowed reciprocally with Ricardo, and occasionally moved across the room to ask the Polish background boy sitting at the opposite corner to lend him felt crayons.

Surjeet's and Amy's patterns of borrowing were more complex. Amy initially did not move much around the classroom to borrow. For some months before the arrangement noted in Figure 4.1, she was seated next to two boys who borrowed reciprocally with her. Later in the year, beginning in February, Amy began to range further afield to borrow. She borrowed even when she had her own materials easily available. She would move around the classroom, lean on the desk of the potential lender and engage him or her in short conversations. She thus continued her friendly and affiliative practices of soliciting connections with other children, despite her physical separation from them. Amy seldom lent anything to others (and was seldom asked to lend anything); on those infrequent occasions when other children used her things, they went into her desk on their own, with her tacit permission, and retrieved the materials themselves.

Surjeet, unlike Amy, was not always a welcome participant in other children's activities. I have already described Mary's occasional hostile initiations with her. From the middle of February, Surjeet sat beside another anglophone girl, Carla, who also was very unfriendly toward her. Carla would rebuff Surjeet's conversational advances and refuse to lend her materials. After a few refusals, Surjeet did not solicit the loan of materials from Carla. However, she often borrowed felt crayons from Mary (who was also occasionally hostile) as well as from Tiffany, seated closer beside her. Surjeet had to move a little away from her desk for borrowing, especially from Mary, but the purpose of her solicitation did not appear primarily to engage the lender in friendly conversation, as it appeared to be with Amy. Rather, Surjeet seemed sometimes fairly tense when borrowing from Mary, as if she thought that her presence or her request might lead to a hostile remark. She was not apparently tense when exchanging materials with Tiffany; these interactions seemed friendly and easy. Surjeet was an enthusiastic lender and was alert to occasions on which children seated near her could use one of her resources. Despite Carla's unfriendliness, Surjeet continued to offer to lend her materials.

The anglophone children also borrowed and lent materials. In particular, it was evident that several of the anglophone boys roamed quite freely around the class on borrowing excursions. The anglophone girls moved less, but their choices about whom to lend to and from whom to solicit loans, like the boys', reflected their changing social allegiances. Items that were particularly attractive were often solicited by many children. The anglophone children who sat at the back of the room often appeared to have the most attractive materials in terms of other children's requests to borrow them.

Evidently the borrowing and lending practices in this classroom reflected the children's social relations. Julie and Martin seldom lent or borrowed; these particular children were also relatively quiet verbal participants in their classroom. Amy borrowed a great deal from other children in what appeared to be attempts to solicit enjoyable affiliations with them. For Surjeet, borrowing and lending were more ambiguous: although she sought often to participate in the practices, they did not appear to lead always to enjoyable interactions with other children. Surjeet's attempts to lend to other children appeared to be attempts to 'buy' acceptability; the fact that children did not often solicit loans from her reinforced her position as subordinate. The anglophone children at the back of the room, on the other hand, had higher status in the children's social relations and they were frequently asked for loans.

Classroom practices of borrowing and lending material resources thus clearly intersected with issues with regard to community participants' social relations. These issues no doubt affected the economics of how other resources of the classroom were managed.

USING YOUR OWN WORDS AND IDEAS

In this Grade 1 classroom, as in many others, the teacher frequently enjoined the children to 'do their own work' and children quickly learned this 'rule' and enforced it themselves.

(7)

Amy is drawing a picture on a piece of paper on Martin's desk.

Ms Reynolds: Oh no, Amy, you're supposed to do that on your own. Everybody needs to do this sheet on their own. I need to know what everybody can do on their own.

(8)

Luke:	Ms Reynolds, can I help Rita?
Ms Reynolds:	No.
	(Luke goes to Rita's desk. He sits on a bench near Rita)
John:	*(classmate next to Rita, to Luke)* Ms Reynolds said no. Luke, I'm keeping my eye on you.

(9)

Linda comes up to teacher who is talking to an aide.

Linda:	Ms Reynolds, Surjeet was helping Tiffany.
Ms Reynolds:	Thank you Linda. Surjeet, do your own work.
	(Pause 10 seconds)
Natalie:	Ms Reynolds, Terry and Amy are looking at our work!
Ms Reynolds:	Maybe you could move.

The teacher's and the children's customary responses to oral 'copying' also exemplified the management of intellectual resources in the classroom. Frequently, Ms Reynolds asked the children individually to speculate on answers to mathematical estimations, or to ask questions or make comments on one another's sharing time contributions. Both the teacher (gently) and the children (often forcefully) made it known that repetitions were illegitimate contributions.

(11)

Natalie shows the class a book she has produced at home.

Natalie:	Any questions or comments?
Surjeet:	You like it?
Natalie:	*(nods)*
May:	How did you make that picture?
Natalie:	Like this.
Amy:	You like that book?
Luke:	We've already had that question, Amy.

(12)

Children estimating how many pumpkin seeds are in the pumpkin. Ms Reynolds writing the numbers on chart next to their names.

Martin:	One zillion.
Ms Reynolds:	I don't know how to write that.
Martin:	One and a lot of zeros.
Ms Reynolds:	Pick a smaller number.
Martin:	One million.

May: One thousand!

Surjeet: One million.

Ms Reynolds: Somebody already guessed that. You can choose a number above or below.

Surjeet turns away.

At the beginning of the year, the focal children often orally repeated like this, but there were no instances after Christmas. Apparently, the children had learned effectively not to repeat in this way.

In kindergarten, some children sometimes used oral and written (drawing) copying as an affiliative practice of flattery. Apparently, their attempts to copy the models of crafts assigned by the teacher were attempts to please. Children would also repeat their friends' statements in language play. If one child drew a picture in a particularly innovative way, several of that child's friends would draw similar pictures and their efforts seemed greeted by the innovator with pleasure. In Grade 1, by contrast, children frequently would huddle over their drawings or written 'stories' in exaggerated attempts to shield their work from the eyes of others. All the children appeared to learn quickly that oral repetitions and copying others' written work were illegitimate.

In this classroom ambiguity surrounded the notion of 'helping'. On the one hand, children helping other children with their tasks was commonly prohibited; children 'helping themselves' (by copying or repeating) was similarly negatively regarded. However, on other occasions, helping was regarded positively. From time to time, Ms Reynolds organised the children in small groups to complete a group task. These group tasks suspended the usual classroom rule of 'doing your own work' and children, not surprisingly, appeared to require some negotiation time, especially at the beginning of such activities, to decide how to manage their contributions. Another task that required helping was associated with journal writing. Before the children wrote in their journals (about their weekend activities, for example), Ms Reynolds encouraged them to speak with an assigned classmate about what they were going to write. Most children refused this help.

In summary, it was apparent that for children to help other children with their tasks was commonly a prohibited practice and that children 'helping themselves' (by copying or repeating) was similarly negatively regarded. 'Helping' was not always so regarded, however, and some tasks were set up explicitly so that children might help each other. However, normally, children were to do 'their own work'.

DISCUSSION

The physical placement of participants in a classroom is one of those everyday practices which 'exhibit, indeed generate the social structures of the relevant domain' (Mehan, 1993: 243). Requiring children to work at desks assigned by the teacher is a very common practice of primary classrooms. In this classroom, the practice obviously controlled which children were in proximity with one another, brought some children under close teacher surveillance, and disrupted verbal inter-actions for some – but not all – of the children. Those children defined as needing help because they were 'ESL', as well as anglophone children perceived to be having some difficulty with school, were so placed as to make chatting between them more difficult than it was for other children. Children perceived to be coping well with the requirements of Grade 1 sat at the back of the room together, further from the teacher; they thus could engage with one another in lengthy, obviously enjoyable conversations.

Postmodern philosophers have made us alert to the purposes and effects of surveillance. Foucault (1979) wrote about 18th century innovations in French education, envisioned by Jean-Baptiste de la Salle, directed toward improving the efficiency of schooling:

> By assigning individual places it made possible the supervision of each indi-vidual and the simultaneous work of all . . . It made the educational space function like a learning machine, but also as a machine for supervising, hierarchising, rewarding. Jean-Baptiste de La Salle dreamt of a classroom in which the spatial distribution might provide a whole series of distinctions at once: according to the pupils' progress, worth, character, application, cleanli-ness and parents' fortune . . . 'Pupils attending the highest lessons will be placed in the benches closest to the wall, followed by the others according to the order of the lessons moving toward the middle of the classroom . . . ' Things must be arranged so that 'those whose parents are neglectful and verminous must be separated from those who are careful and clean; that an unruly and frivolous pupil should be placed between two who are well-behaved and serious . . . ' (Foucault, 1979: 147)

Foucault observed that classroom spatial arrangements that place individuals in separate locations – facilitating supervision, hierarchy and rewards – historically trace to about the time of the Industrial Revolution in Europe. Perpetual observation of individuals under this system provided for the establishment of norms and rank:

> In the eighteenth century, 'rank' begins to define the great form of distribution of individuals in the educational order: rows or ranks of pupils in the class, corri-dors, courtyards; rank attributed to each pupil at the end of each task and each examination; the rank he obtains from week to week, month to month, year to year (Foucault, 1979: 146–7).

As Ryan (1989) noted with regard to the same period:

> [W]orkers, prisoners, patients, students and citizens were compared, differenti-ated, and ranked according to where they stood in relation to the 'good' and the 'bad' . . . [S]anctions were universally employed to 'normalise' deviants who by their actions departed from accepted standards. (Ryan, 1989: 400)

Perhaps students who enter school speaking languages other than English are defined as something like 'benignly deviant', in Foucault's terms, in that their language departs from accepted standards and that as a group they constitute a rank requiring normalisation. McDermott (1993) and Mehan (1993) both pointed out the ways in which the rank of 'learning disabled' has a reality in public schools independent of the individuals assigned to the rank. Thinking about ESL status as a similar rank, requiring normalisation, could help in disrupting our taken-for-granted notions of what learning a second language in schools comprises.

The children whose desks were placed close to the teacher's customary position in the class were seen as appropriately interacting only or at least primarily with the teacher and then working on their own in the completion of teacher-assigned tasks. When Amy and Surjeet were removed from the class for ESL instruction, they came under the very close supervision of another teacher, as members of a much smaller group of children. In this way, relative to the children whom the teacher saw as capable students, the focal children had relatively few unobstructed (or unsupervised) opportunities to speak with peers, including more experienced users of English. Children sitting at the front of the room legitimately interacted only with the teacher. In one way, this might been seen as facilitating their second language learning – in interacting primarily with the most expert 'old-timer' (in English) in the room. Shuy (1981) pointed out a particular difficulty with this arrangement, however, noting the sociolinguistic inappropriateness of students speaking like teachers.

Amy's and Surjeet's voluntary removal of themselves from large group sessions, combined with their removal from the class for ESL pullout, contributed to the impression of their increasing 'marginalisation'. 'Marginalisation' is the customary, but in this case rather inapt, metaphor. In truth, being on the margins, farther from teacher surveillance, in some ways could put a child in a more powerful position; one had more autonomy in choosing one's own activities and verbal participation than when one was more centrally located with regard to the teacher. Amy's and Surjeet's removal of themselves to their desks might, therefore, have been a practice of resistance to the centrally defined classroom activities.

A second practice had to do with individual management of material resources. The children had desks in which they stored their individually purchased materials; they were to use their own materials, bring their own books and so on. For a variety of reasons, many children did not always have available individually the resources they needed for task completion, and so they borrowed from other students. Borrowing subverted in some ways the intent of the first classroom practice: keeping children in their separate desks. Roaming for borrowing was risky, because the teacher could and did stop the children from doing so and reprimanded them for it, and because other children could legitimately complain about it. The performance of this borrowing practice reinforced the lesson that some children had more resources than others, that some had 'better' resources than others, and that individual children had the power to decide whether or not they would share their resources. Lending was not stigmatised; borrowing was. In addition, of course, children learned that although it was not a teacher-legitimated practice, they could engage in borrowing surreptitiously.

Finally, both the teacher and the children enforced the practice of requiring that children not copy one another's written or verbal productions. Throughout the year, all the children became more physically vigilant about protecting their written productions from others. At the beginning of the year, the focal children more frequently copied (repeated) other children's verbal productions than did anglophone children. By the end of the year, very little of this kind of verbal copying took place. Its unequivocally negative valuation might have been responsible for its disappearance. Learners of English in this classroom, discouraged from explicit appropriation of others' words, were taught that words, like things, were individually owned and were not community resources.

Lave and Wenger (1991: 31) wrote that 'learning is an integral and inseparable aspect of social practice'; what did these children learn in these three social practices? These classroom practices, so commonplace as to be almost invisible, contribute to instantiating the notion that the children's individuality must be established, reinforced and protected. Children sit in their own desks, use their own materials, do their own work and use their own words. Knowing and staying in one's place, having good materials in one's own place, keeping track of and taking care of them oneself, having one's own 'things' to write and draw and say, establish each child as an individual, who, on her own, negotiates classroom life. Identity practices operate so that the community learns to see some children as more or less privileged with regard to their acquisitions and more or less autonomous in deciding their activities and verbal participation.

In the same way that a child may have more or fewer crayons in her desk than another, these economic practices contribute to some children being seen by the whole community as having more or less English, literacy, mathematics, or whatever in their heads than others. Teachers ascertain how much of what any individual child's head contains and report that to parents and authorities. In the Grade 1 classroom, I noted the teacher's particularly frequent reminders to children to work on their own just before report cards were written and distributed.

Lave and Wenger's (1991: 49) discussion of learning as participation in communities of practice offers a way to 'extend . . . the study of learning beyond the context of pedagogical structuring, includ[e] the structure of the social world in the analysis, and tak[e] into account in a central way the conflictual nature of social practice'. If one takes such a perspective on this classroom, it is a community whose practices construct children as individuals and their acquisitions as personal belongings.

This individualising of the children starts a process of community stratification which increasingly leads to the exclusion of some students from certain activities, practices, identities and affiliations. Schools 'break them up/take them away'. First language subcommunities do not survive; second language learners become systematically excluded from just those conversations in which they might legitimately peripherally participate with child experts, English old-timers. They cannot speak like teachers, but those are the only experts with whom they are to interact legitimately. In a stratified community in which the terms of stratification become increasingly visible to all, some students become defined as deficient; this systematically excludes them from just those practices in which they might otherwise appropriate identities and practices of growing competence and expertise.

Of course, many other practices of classrooms and their wider context reinforce the notion that individuals come to own knowledge. Certainly, the practices of those researchers who have investigated second language learning, as well as most educational psychologists (as discussed by Wertsch, 1991), contribute as well to reinforcing this notion. The three locally observable practices identified here contributed to the beginning of a process by which children from minority language backgrounds began to acquire school identities as persons whose 'inventory' was smaller than the inventories of others. They began to acquire identities which, in some very problematic and contradictory ways, were seen to require normalising.

The focal children were, at this time, six and seven years old. Any long-term effects of their positioning in their Grade 1 classroom are impossible to determine. Nevertheless, a Toronto secondary student, a Japanese learner of ESL, has expresssed a disturbing possible future for these children:

> You go to [a non-ESL class] and sit with white people. You understand the content of the class, but when you have to find a partner and work on a group project, you can't get into a group. You feel too embarrassed to ask someone to be your partner. You feel like you're gonna be a burden on them. So you don't ask them; you wait until they ask you. (Kanno & Applebaum, 1995: 40)

Kanno and Applebaum (1995: 41) also cite research (Brislin,1981; Furnham & Bochner, 1986; Klein *et al.*, 1971) that shows 'that many students from the Far East have difficulty developing a viable social network with North Americans'. My research suggests that the everyday, almost invisible practices of classrooms, beginning very early, contribute to these long-term effects.

Reversal of these effects will not be a simple matter of putting the children back together again. As Kanno and Applebaum (1995: 43) remark, 'Perhaps it is high time we discarded our romantic notion that if we put children of all ethnic/linguistic backgrounds in one place we will witness the development of true cross-cultural understanding'. Mary's racist comments about birthday parties serve as a reminder that patterns of exclusion and domination persist. Paley (1992) described her attempts to build resistance to 'habits of rejection' by instituting the classroom rule for children, 'You can't say you can't play'. She observed in her classroom work that some children were positioned as outsiders and she observed:

> The [traditional] approach has been to help the outsiders develop the character-istics which will make them more acceptable to the insiders. I am suggesting something different: The group must change its attitudes and expectations toward those who, for whatever reasons, are not yet part of the system. (Paley, 1992: 33)

Certainly the approach in the education of children who go to North American schools speaking languages other than the majority language has been to attempt to help them 'develop the characteristics [the language] which will make them more acceptable to insiders'. Paley asked how to make those insider groups more inclu-sive, that is, how the group can change to allow those outsiders in? Freire sees the problem of outsider/insider somewhat differently:

> The truth is that the oppressed are not 'marginals', are not people living 'out-side' society. They have always been 'inside' – inside the structure which made them 'beings for others'. The solution is not to 'integrate' them into the structure of oppression, but to transform that structure so that they can become 'beings for themselves'. (Friere, 1970: 55)

This perspective, which sees educational structures (communities/practices) as particularly oppressive to some, is perhaps more critical than is customary in SLA literature.

Packer (1993) cited Cazden's (1993) argument that coming 'to "participate" in a linguistic community is not . . . a process without conflict: it involves the meeting and clash of divergent interests and the points of view to which these interests give rise' (Packer, 1993: 259). As speakers struggle to appropriate the voices of others and to 'bend' those voices to their own purposes, they are also struggling to appro-priate the identity positions expressed by those voices, and to 'bend' those identities to their own purposes. As Hull and Rose put it:

> A fundamental social and psychological reality about discourse – oral or written – is that human beings continually appropriate each other's language to establish group membership, to grow and to define themselves . . . [Our own] clearly documented writing may let us forget or even, camouflage how much more it is that we borrow from existing texts, how much we depend on member-ship in a community for our language, our voices, our very arguments. (Hull & Rose, 1989: 151–2)

However, in a stratified community, those from whom words and positions are appropriated may resist their appropriation, denying the legitimacy of those words and those positions in other people's mouths and bodies. Much SLA research has assessed how individual second language learners move progressively (and more or less quickly) toward more extensive acquisition of the second language and (hence, assumedly), fuller participation in the activities of the second language community. Nevertheless, the practices of the particular community documented here appear in effect to prevent the increasing empowerment and active participation of some of those defined as second language learners. Coming to understand how research practices, as well as classroom practices have collaborated in constructing ESL students as individuals who, on their own, acquire or do not acquire the capital of the classroom (the language) may go some way to help find alternative practices that will permit those students to become and be seen as 'beings for themselves'.

Clearly, we must understand how to transform the social structures in the milieux for which we have responsibility – classroom – so as to prepare our students effectively for the conflicts to which Cazden referred. Investigation of the social practices in those situations must be ongoing, critical and broad.

Notes

1. Concerned about the safety of video-tapes of children, Harvey's parents asked that he not be observed or taped in Grade 1. So, although he was enrolled in the Grade 1 classroom, he was not a focus of observation there.
2. These six 'ESL' children received instruction from the specialist ESL teacher, who removed them from their classroom for this specialist support. All the children who had been enrolled in the kindergarten Language Development class were tested at the end of kindergarten with regard to their English language proficiency, as described in Chapter 3. On the basis of this test, the assessor had decided that only Amy and Surjeet of the focal children required specialist ESL support.
3. Early in the school year, one of the children in the classroom was diagnosed with head lice. Children's desks were moved further away from one another for a couple of weeks, though in the same arrangement, in an attempt to inhibit the spread of the mites. This arrangement really 'spread out' the children. Later, the desks were moved closer together so that adjoining desks were touching one another (as illustrated in Figure 4.1).
4. In June, the teacher moved a Cantonese-speaking girl behind Amy, but she had not been placed there previously. Except for the movement of this girl, Figure 4.1 shows the placement of children from the end of February to the end of June.
5. Typical of their sometimes apparently difficult interactions was this recorded in March:
    Martin: Ricardo, where you got your ruler?
    Ricardo: (*Pause 5 seconds*) I got this from store. (*shows 'action figure'*)
    Martin: NO! (*angry, loud*) Ruler!
    Ricardo goes to back of room.
6. Randy's family moved away from the catchment area of Suburban School when he was in Grade 1 and I observed him until the end of Grade 1 at his new school, which was not far from Suburban School and had a similar ethnic and linguistic mix. Although Mrs Reynolds was sorry to lose him, as she believed that Randy was one of the 'brightest' children in her class, his teacher at his new school told me in an interview in February

that he was 'the most dramatically affected ESL child [she] had ever taught' and that she was 'referring him for learning assistance' because she was convinced he had some very serious learning disability. Randy was observably very quiet in his new classroom. The referral in fact never happened, probably due to his teacher requiring a medical leave shortly after this conversation. Randy's next teacher was not so concerned about him; by the end of the year, Randy was evaluated as developing 'normally' and as being only slightly handicapped by his 'ESL-ness'.

CHAPTER 5

Discursive Practices in Grade 2 Language Arts Lessons

> The challenge for ESL teachers . . . is to recognise that classroom relationships and interactions both consciously and unconsciously define what is desirable and possible for newcomers. (Morgan, 1997: 433)

In September 1996, Martin, Julie, Amy and Surjeet were enrolled in Mrs Larson's Grade 2 class, along with 10 children classified as learners of ESL and 8 children designated as English speakers. This classroom was somewhat bigger than the Grade 1 classroom; desks were placed together in 'pods' of four or five. Mrs Larson, in consultation with the children, changed seating arrangements every two weeks or so. Mrs Larson was in her sixth year of teaching, and had spent all six years at Suburban School.

During the summer vacation between Grade 1 and Grade 2, Julie's family had begun to have serious difficulties with regard to their immigration status and were threatened with deportation. Because they were resisting the deportation, they did not know whether or when they would be required to leave Canada. As it happened, they were deported from Canada in June of the next year. Amy had spent some of the summer in Hong Kong with her parents and her grandmother; her parents were considering where they would live after the repatriation of Hong Kong to China in July 1997. Martin's family reported that their summer had been 'relatively uneventful' and that both Martin and his brother (who was about to enter Grade 1) were looking forward to school. Surjeet's grandparents had returned from an extended trip to India over the summer and they reported to Karen Dhaliwal-Rai that they had begun to be 'active in assisting [Surjeet and two cousins] in completing homework and additional work that the grandfather feels is needed for their learning'.

I interviewed Mrs Larson early in the school year (in October) about the focal children as they entered her classroom. The following are excerpts from that interview:

(1)

> Julie's doing okay. She's average Grade 2 in reading . . . Her spelling is not very good and I'm having a hard time getting her to study . . . Verbally she does well. I'm pleased with her verbal communication. There's some problems at home, immigration problems. They will have to go back to Poland and she was born here. And she's upset about this . . . In my opinion, she's progressed, but it's been small . . .
>
> Amy is doing well. I noticed that her language is really coming up since the beginning of the year . . . She's a bright little girl . . . She had a lot of trouble focusing at the beginning of this year, too busy watching the other kids [but] she's really come around . . . She does her work and she does it well.
>
> Martin does well, his reading is also average Grade 2 . . . Martin is a very bright boy. He's also very single minded and [his] Mum has expressed some concern about this. Martin seems to move to the beat of his own drum.
>
> Surjeet continues to have difficulties with reading, spelling and even a little bit of oral language. However, I don't feel it's necessarily an ESL problem, I think Surjeet is just low . . . She's limited in just what she can absorb and in what she can understand and I think that's going to dog her all her life . . .

During this school year, Sarah Yip and I and occasionally Elaine Day observed the children weekly during one of their Language Arts lessons, which were frequently approximately 80 minutes in length. In many of the lessons children completed written work, usually as the penultimate activity (the teacher's checking student work being the final activity). However, rather than the written work children produced in these lessons, here I focus on the oral discourse practices of these lessons.

I consider here how the oral discursive practices of these lessons allowed the focal children to appropriate classroom language. In Chapters 2 and 3, I examined identity practices; in Chapter 4, I examined resource distribution practices, and for each I analyzed effects on children's access to classroom language. This chapter focuses on discourse practices and how well they provide the focal children with access to appropriating powerful and desirable voices in their community. Examining how these discourse practices are organised allows a somewhat different perspective on how classroom practices enable certain social relations and ultimately learning.

LANGUAGE ARTS LESSONS

In a 1988 review of research on classroom discourse, Cazden pointed out two predominant kinds of social organisation in elementary schools in the United

Kingdom and the United States: large group instruction ('with the teacher in control at the front of the room') and individualised instruction ('with children working alone on assigned tasks, and the teacher monitoring and checking their individual progress') (Cazden, 1998: 124). Most of the Language Arts lessons we observed were organised around large group and individualised instruction, with the addition of some small group and partner conversations. The following activity pattern was typical:

(1) Presentation of a common experience to the whole group of children (e.g. teacher reading a storybook to the children or teacher and children viewing a video-tape).
(2) Whole group discussion of the above event (sometimes this discussion itself was the common experience) in the form of 'recitation sequences'.
(3) Teacher-mandated partner or small group conversations between or among children about the topic under discussion (common, but not in every lesson, and not always in the same place in the lesson sequence).
(4) Individual completion of a written exercise by children at their desks, with children talking with one another about the task at hand, and/or about other matters (student-managed conversations).
(5) Examination and evaluation of individual children's work by the teacher.

In this chapter, I examine in most detail the three central oral discourse activities (whole group discussions, teacher-mandated partner and small group conversations, and student-managed conversations). For each of these, I consider (a) the purposes of the discourse structure, (b) the positional possibilities the structure offers to interactants, and (c) the possibilities the structure offers to interactants to appropriate voices for themselves and thus to create meaning.

Wells (1993) discussed in detail how particular discourse sequences might be distinguished one from another based on their 'goals' or motives, adapting Leontiev's (1981) formulation of activity theory. He illustrated a variety of goals a teacher could have in engaging in instructional discourse with students. Earlier, Hymes (1972) pointed out the complexity of the construct of speech act purposes, noting that community and individual goals for any particular interaction might vary, and that there might be distinctions between the conventionally expected or ascribed goals of an interaction and the latent or unintended goals. I intend to discuss purpose both in terms of the teacher's and the conventionally recognised, expected and ostensible goals outcomes of each practice, as well as latent or unintended outcomes. Examining teachers' intentions for these practices, students' intentions, and observers' ideas about what purposes the practices serve, might enhance our understandings of what goes on in classrooms.

As well as purposes, I examine how each practice sets up for students positions *vis-à-vis* one another and the teacher. All discourse practices set up particular kinds of social relations between participants. Citing Bakhtin (1981), Hall comments:

> Our every use of language . . . serves as a sociopolitical statement indicating our stance toward the particular interactive moment, our place in that interaction and our positioning toward the others involved. (Hall, 1995: 214).

The particular kinds of positioning possibilities that classroom discourse practices set up are also centrally related to the possibilities they present for students to develop classroom voices.

Finally, the discourse practices of the Language Arts lessons constrain or enable appropriation of voices for the children, for them to express meanings from their own points of view. Bakhtin believed that speakers construct their messages in response to the utterances of others, and that the discursive as well as the social and political contexts of utterances might be seen as joint 'producers' of utterances with their human speakers. For him, speakers are able to make words 'their own' when they are able to adapt them to 'their own semantic and expressive intention' (Bakhtin, 1981: 293). This expression of 'one's own' meanings is, for Bakhtin, the construction of a 'voice', 'a perspective, a conceptual horizon, intention and world view' (Wertsch, 1991: 51). I wish to examine, therefore, how each of the three discourse practices enabled the construction of voice in this classroom.

RECITATION SEQUENCES

Background

Many researchers have noted the commonality in classrooms of three-part recitation sequence formats (also termed triadic dialogue, IRE – Initiation, Response, Evaluation, IRF – Initiation, Response, Follow-up), in which typically, a teacher asks a question, a student responds and the teacher evaluates or follows up on the student's response in some way. Cazden (1988: 29), for example, described this as 'the most common pattern of classroom discourse at all grade levels'. Edwards and Westgate (1994) called the pattern 'the deep grooves along which most classroom talk seems to run'[1] and Wells (1993: 2) noted that 'in some primary classrooms it has been found to be the dominant mode in which the teacher converses'. Many researchers have examined this discursive practice and have variously evaluated it. Some (Mercer, 1992; Newman *et al.*, 1989) have seen it as a practice well-designed to accomplish the educational goals of transmitting information and monitoring children's understanding or internalisation of it. Others (Edwards & Westgate, 1994; Gutierrez & Larson, 1994; MacLure & French, 1981; Wood, 1992) saw the practice as involving children somewhat trivially in a type of 'oral cloze' test in which they merely contribute to meanings constructed by the teacher. Wells (1993: 3) argued that the practice is 'neither good nor bad', observing that it serves important educational purposes of 'cultural reproduction', but that it might not be so effective at engendering 'cultural renewal and [. . .] the formation and empowerment of individual[s]'. He examined several enactments of the sequence in a classroom in which a teacher's varying goals for the practice entailed varying outcomes in students' possibilities for expressing meanings and for co-constructing knowledge with their teacher. In this chapter, I wish to examine how the practice occurred in Mrs Larson's Grade 2 classroom and how it seemed to affect the focal children's possibilities for access to voice there.

Recitation sequences and the focal children

Surjeet reluctantly performed in recitation sequences, and judging by the number of times she volunteered, more reluctantly at the end of the year than at the beginning. She was commonly nominated by Mrs Larson,[2] although rarely by other children (part of the conventions of the classroom: nominated children could nominate other children in an 'I need help' move). Typical of her performance was the following: in March, after groups of children had presented reports on planets in the solar system, Mrs Larson opened a discussion of what would be essential for the establishment of human communities on these planets. Two children volunteered 'air' and 'food'; Mrs Larson then asked Surjeet (without Surjeet bidding to answer) for another essential:

(2)

Mrs L:	So we need air and we need food. What else is super important to have on that space ship? *Many children bidding to answer. Not Surjeet, though.* Surjeet, what would <u>you</u> want to have on that space ship? *(Pause 6 seconds)*[3] *Surjeet is mouthing words, not saying anything audible. She is looking down.* Maybe it's something you're taking to your new planet. What would you want? *(Pause 11 seconds)* *Surjeet looks down.* You've got air to breathe, and you've got your 'Shreddies' to eat, what else would you need. *(Pause 21 seconds)* *Surjeet looks at ceiling, looks to the right, starts mouthing words again, but doesn't say anything audible.* What else would you need? What would be really important to have with you? *(Pause 4 seconds)*
Surjeet:	A space ship?
Mrs L:	Well, you all, what we're talking about is what would be *on* that space ship with you. Now think along that line. You're on the right track.
Surjeet:	Fire.
Mrs L:	You want fire?
Surjeet:	On the out, outside.

Mrs L: You want fire outside the spaceship? So the space ship can go?
Surjeet nods.
Okay, but I'm thinking of something that you would pack inside.
Something you would need to take inside the space ship. Something
you might need on the other planet.
Surjeet: M:::*(Looking around, shifting.)*
Mrs L: We've got air. Remember some of those planets don't have air. So
we've got air. The air in the space ship. And we have food. What else
would you need?
(Pause 5 seconds)
*Surjeet is looking down. Many children raise their hands, and Mrs
Larson addresses them.*
I'm sorry, she hasn't asked for help. I don't know why your hands are
up. Thank you.
(Pause 7 seconds)
Surjeet is mouthing words.
Either pass or ask for help, dear.
Surjeet: Pass.

In this sequence Mrs Larson attempted repeatedly to scaffold Surjeet's answer.
She summarised ('You've got air to breathe and you've got your 'Shreddies' to eat.
What else would you need?'), made leading remarks ('Something you might need
on another planet . . . ') and waited a long time for Surjeet to answer. Despite this,
Surjeet remained silent. Surjeet frequently responded with silence when called on in
this way. In interviews, Mrs Larson referred to this throughout the year. In March,
she said:

(3)

> I truly believe Surjeet is doing as well as she is going to do. She's very very
> hesitant about answering questions. I try to ask her when her hand is up.
> Unfortunately her hand is rarely up. It's just come to the point now where she
> would just rather relax. I will ask her and my thing is, you have to try, and I
> know this embarrasses her sometimes but I have to get across to her that she
> has to make the effort. But she'll sit there and she'll sit there and I say, it's
> okay, Surjeet, but you have to answer, you do have to give some answer, we'll
> help you. As I said [in an earlier statement in which she remarked that
> Surjeet might have learning limitations], this is as good as it's going to get for
> Surjeet.

Martin also rarely bid for the position of respondent in recitation sequences;
however, Mrs Larson nominated him much less than she did Surjeet. In one lesson in
April, however, he did volunteer more frequently and participate more actively.
Early in the lesson, Mrs Larson was asking the children for the names of food groups
and for examples of food falling in these groups. After a child had volunteered

'crackers' belonging to the bread and cereals group, Mrs Larson asked the children why this food might belong in that group.

(4)

Agatha:	Because I think they're made out of like um bread dough and [I think something
Mrs L:	[They're made from flour, yes. Same thing that bread is made from. But you add different ingredients to get bread. So, uh, that's why it's in the bread and cereals. What are some of those other things? Can you tell me about another food that would be found in the group? My, not too many people are thinking today. I hardly see any hands up. Martin?
Martin:	The Egg Waffles?[4]
Mrs L:	*(To Martin)* How do you know they are <u>egg</u> waffles? *(To whole group)* You don't know what kind of waffles they are so you just have to say waffles. Yes. Why are they in that group, Martin?
Martin:	Uh:: *(Pause 13 seconds)* *Jean Paul puts up his hand with a loud intake of breath.*
Mrs L:	He hasn't asked for help, Jean Paul. Hand down please. Why would waffles be in the bread and cereal group?
Martin:	Uh::: *(Pause 13 seconds)* They are made out of *(playing with his shirt collar, tapping his chin)*
Mrs L:	A little louder sweetie.
Martin:	Because they are made, they are made out of *(Pause 3 seconds)* flour?
Mrs L:	Yes, sure. There is a lot of flour in them. You mix them with egg and a few other ingredients.

In this example, Mrs Larson waited for Martin to answer for almost half a minute in all. She protected Martin's turn ('He hasn't asked for help, Jean Paul') suggesting that there is importance in Martin giving the answer, not in the answer being available for the group discussion of 'breads and cereals'.

Amy and Julie more frequently performed in recitation sequences than the other two focal children. In a lesson on 'multiculturalism' in January, Mrs Larson read the children a story book about multiculturalism and then elicited from them their ideas about 'what makes up culture'. The children had offered 'music' and 'food', and Mrs Larson continued to question them. On this occasion, Sarah Yip was observing; just before the following excerpt, Amy had come up to Sarah and whispered in Cantonese some question that Sarah was not able to make out.

(5)

While Mrs Larson is talking, Amy has risen and come over to me [Sarah], and whispers in Chinese. I can't hear much of what she said so I shake my head. Amy looks back at Mrs L. I open my eyes questioningly at Amy. She opens her eyes and looks at me.

Mrs L:	Let's just go over what we've discussed with this class, please. We've talked about culture is the language that a different people speak, it's a thing they listen to, it's the clothes they wear. It's the food they eat. Anything else? Anything else? Amy, anything else you want to add?
Amy:	The colour of your um, body.
Mrs L:	Well:: not really. Not really. I could, uh be born and raised in a culture where the people looked quite different from me but it would still be my culture because I listen to that music. I eat that food. I dress that way. So the way you look doesn't have as much to do with culture as all those other things. But you often associate the way people look with a certain culture, you're right there.

Later in the sequence, Amy again offered 'hair colours', with Mrs Larson responding similarly to above. She continued:

(6)

Mrs L:	Think about something else, Amy. We've got clothes, music, foods. What else? What else makes up culture? All the things we read and talked about. You and I were just talking about one of those things. When you came to Canada you had to learn? (*Pause 3 seconds*) You weren't born in Canada, were you? When you came to school you had to learn? (*Pause 5 seconds*) What did you learn at school?
Amy:	Learn things.
Mrs L:	Yes, you had to learn a lot of things, but before you could learn those things you had to be able to do what with all the children and the teacher? Oh I'm sorry, Leo. I'm talking to Amy now and you know better. And I don't want to see that again. (*Pause 6 seconds*) You've never thought hard about it. If you can't figure it out you can pass or ask for help.
Amy:	Um::
Mrs L:	Right. Can you ask for help?
Amy:	Agatha.
Agatha:	Dancing.

Mrs L: OK, it's not quite what I was thinking of, but definitely we can put
dance down. What else can we put down here? Peter?

Peter: Language.

Mrs L: Language, yes. Did – you had to learn English. Amy. Amy, listen
please. You had to learn English so you can talk – communicate with
each other ** you can hear ***. Language.
(To all the children) Something else that makes up culture?

Amy had raised a complicated issue (the relation of race to culture) and Mrs
Larson tried to acknowledge and address Amy's answer while moving the
sequence along. But she had difficulty eliciting from Amy the item she (Mrs
Larson) needed, 'language', so as to construct the relatively sophisticated but
personal answer she wished to give to Amy. Most teachers would recognise the
difficulty Mrs Larson had in this sequence, knowing that constructing questions so
that children will supply the linguistic items needed to move the discourse along in
ways the teacher intends is not always particularly easy. Agatha's 'dancing' is a
good example of the problem: she answered a previous question accurately with
this item, but it didn't help Mrs Larson construct the meaning she wanted to
develop.

TEACHER-MANDATED PARTNER AND SMALL GROUP CONVERSATIONS

Background

Asking students to discuss something with a partner or a small group, is a fairly
common classroom practice and, has been often recommended for second language
classrooms (Long, *et al.*, 1976; Long, 1977, 1981; Long & Porter, 1985; Pica &
Doughty, 1986). Recognising that large group formats give students limited opportunities for language practice, many educators have claimed that small group work
allows students more turns at talk in conditions of relative power equality with other
interlocutors (Pica, 1987).

In the Language Arts lessons, the timing of teacher-mandated conversations
between peers varied. Sometimes, the teacher asked the children to speak with partners or small groups during short breaks while listening to stories – to speculate on
the motives of characters, on possible plot outcomes, and so on. She also set up small
group or partner conversations at the end of a story or videotape. Sometimes she
interrupted a whole class discussion to get the children to engage in partner or small
group discussion for 'brainstorming' and so on. How the focal children engaged in
these conversations and the possibilities they seemed to offer the children for
constructing classroom voices are the foci here.

Teacher-mandated peer conversations and the focal children

Peer conversations mandated by the teacher sometimes allowed the children the opportunity to express their own meanings in apparently enjoyable ways, although not always. For example, in a February lesson centred around reading a children's book, *Ming Lo Moves the Mountain* (Lobel, 1982), Mrs Larson stopped reading after every page or so and asked the children to discuss with a partner what might come next in the story. Amy and a classmate Mary (in whose home only English was used) engaged in an apparently lively and pleasurable conversation:

(7)

Mary:	With the um woods on your head and the mountain would move far far away and you could dig and build your house again.
Amy:	***
Mary:	Yup.
Amy:	Okay, so that wise man said that.
Mary:	And that wise man was covered in smoke so they can't see him *Both girls giggle.*
Amy:	Yeah, the wise man sticks glue like this to your feet and put a log on your head and
Mary:	No, like put the logs of your house on, no on [over your head and hold them and close your eyes
Amy:	[over your head and hold them and close your eyes
Mary:	[And keep on doing this for many hours
Amy:	[And keep on doing this for many hours And the mountain will go away, far far away
Mary:	So they can build the house again. *Mary is squatting, The girls join hands and start to bounce, each word in the next utterance corresponds with a bounce.* But -they -did -not- say -that- so -I -think- it- will- not- work.
Amy:	I think it <u>will</u> work.
Mary:	Well *(rising intonation)* I think it will work too. Uh, I gotta get up.
Mrs L:	And stop, please.

Birdwhistell (1970), in an extended study of 'kinesics' (body motion and communication) points out that conversations can be like 'dances', and Amy's and Mary's non-verbal behaviour here looked pleasurable, coordinated and a lot like a 'dance'. When Mary began her 'But-they-did-not-' utterance, the girls held hands and bounce together on their heels. Both girls contributed to the conversation, indeed, several parts were completed chorally (although Mary's seems the 'lead' voice in this chorus). Despite Mary's longer experience with speaking English, Amy did not hesitate to disagree with her about whether 'it will work'. The girls were able in this excerpt to 'play' in their response and to build together a collaborative response to the teacher's prompt.

The 'Ming Lo' conversation prompt also elicited very animated conversation between Martin and his partner, Jean Paul. Jean Paul's family were from Quebec and they used French in their home. Jean Paul received ESL specialist support in his Grade 2 classroom. He had many health problems in Grade 2 and missed a great deal of school. Early in the reading of the story, when none of the children knew very much about the story's plot, Mrs Larson prompted the children to engage in partner conversation concerning what had already happened in the story:

(8)

Martin speaking to Jean Paul before teacher has finished giving students instructions for the exercise. Martin looks happy and makes many hand and arm movements throughout his first utterance.

Martin:	*** When, when, um, Ming Lo tries to move the mountain, he looks down and he sees a lamp, he sees a dirty *(*rubs his hands around as if he is rubbing a lamp*) A genie comes out of it. 'I wish that this mountain would be crushed to pieces!' And he crushes it to pieces. Then he * *(More arm and hand movements).* Your turn.
Jean Paul:	What?
	(pause 3 seconds)
	Oh, there was a big hole *(he traces a circle on the rug)* There's lots of things *(his hands are moving around as if he is drawing things in the air)* and he jumps and splats, oh:: ** *(more vocalisations, probably not words. Smiles, Martin smiles and moves with Jean Paul)*
Martin:	Hey, I know! When there's a puppy when **
Jean Paul:	Wuh, wuh, wuh * big nose and then he goes *(again lots of hand and arm movements)*
Martin:	He goes like this *(makes a biting and then spitting motion)*

Although Mrs Larson had asked the children to tell what had already happened in the story, Martin and Jean Paul interpreted the partner set-up as an invitation to imagine a story. Their stories bore little relation plot-wise to the story the teacher has started to read. Martin's story resembled a plot from a then-popular American children's movie, while Jean Paul's story was difficult to interpret. However, both appeared to have fun playing together in the composing of the stories. Both of them joyfully engaged in a partly verbal, partly vocalic, largely bodily-enacted creation of two narratives. They had pleasurable 'places' in this task, and had access to each other as resources in it. Martin and Jean Paul's interaction affirmed both as story-tellers, despite the fact that much of their stories was accomplished non-verbally, and bore little relation to the story the teacher had just read.

Partner and small group conversations sometimes facilitated access to community knowledge resources, but not always. As part of the Canada's Food Guide lesson described earlier (Excerpt 4), Mrs Larson paired children with others and had them interview each other about their favourite food in each food group, so as to complete a worksheet. She had given general instructions on how to complete the sheet to the whole class. Julie and Amy had begun their interviews; Mrs Larson walked by where they were sitting:

(9)

Mrs L:	Girls, you have to do this section too. *(pointing to their sheets)*
Julie:	I know, we are.
Mrs L:	Okay.
Julie:	Cause we don't get it very much.
Mrs L:	Pardon?
Julie:	We don't get it.
Mrs L:	You don't understand what to do?
	Julie shakes her head and looks down.
	Okay, you're going to say to Amy, 'Amy, what's your favourite grain product? What is your favourite thing from the bread and cereal group?'
Julie:	Cereal?
Mrs L:	No, no, I'm asking Amy. See you would ask Amy this.
Amy:	Cereal.
Mrs L:	Do you like um, so you like your morning cereal? That's your favourite thing? Okay, then you would put down cereal. *(pointing to Julie)* Don't worry about your spelling. That's a girl. And now, Amy, you ask Julie what her favourite thing from the grain products or bread and cereal group is. Maybe she likes bran muffins the best. Maybe she like waffles the best, I don't know, you ask her. And you write it down. *(Mrs L leaves)*
Amy:	Uh what's your favourite, um
Julie:	[vegetable or grain
Amy:	[vegetable or grain – products.
Julie:	Um::::.
Amy:	Did you know how to write cereal?
Julie:	I know it's up there but I can't look. *(gestures to the board upon which is the Canada Food Guide poster)*
Amy:	C-E, C-E makes S sound.
Julie:	'Kay, um, waffles.
Amy:	Waffles? *(tries to write this down. Julie leans closer.)*
Julie:	/w::ɔ::: / *(J. helping A. 'sound it out')*
Julie:	Ok, now, Amy, what is your veg, favourite vegetable and fruit?
Amy:	Um, apple.

Julie:	Apple is fruit. Do you like bananas?
Amy:	Well, um, sometimes . . . . *(looks away)*
Julie:	They're good for you.
Amy:	The yellow ones.
Julie:	Okay, I'll print banana, okay?
Amy:	Okay.
Julie:	/b::: æ::::n::::::æ::::n:::æ::/ *(as she writes it)* There's banana.
Amy:	*(leans in toward Julie)* Those, those apples makes your teeth, when you teeth is wob, wobb, um, really like moving when you move it, push it. Like when you eat apple, it will fall in, into the apple and you will eat the tooth.
Julie:	*(smiles very briefly)* 'Kay, now you ask me.
Amy:	What's your favourite vegetable or fruit? Fruit?
Julie:	Mmmm. I like, I like um apple.

In this excerpt, Mrs Larson explicitly coached Amy and Julie in the language they were to use to accomplish the task. Although she then left, she had set up the speech acts in which the girls subsequently engaged. The worksheet also structured their verbal activity. Julie, in particular, seemed to regard Mrs Larson's instructions and the worksheet as mandating her verbal behaviour. The girls were noticeably physically disengaged from one another during this conversation. Both spend a good deal of the time looking away and twisting their bodies away from one another. Amy moved in closer to Julie during her apples- can-make-you-swallow-your-teeth turn, but Julie was looking away from Amy. When Amy finished this utterance, Julie smiled very quickly, not looking at Amy, and said, ''Kay, now you ask me'. The girls collaborated to some extent in this conversation: They said 'vegetable or grain' in chorus, helped one another spell the words, and they cued one another about asking the questions. However, on the whole, they did not really speculate about their own meanings or create knowledge together. Negotiations of power relations between them were only subtly manifested here, but Julie rather easily persuaded Amy that she should choose bananas as her favourite fruit and vegetable rather than apples, and she ignored Amy's conversational gambit about how apples can make you swallow a loose tooth. Julie took the role of teacher or leader in this exchange; consequently, parts of the conversation resemble a recitation sequence. Despite their status equality as children and the fact that mistakes here were inconsequential, the girls did not stray very far from the set task. Amy's attempt to speculate beyond the sheet got nowhere.

Amy and Julie's conversation was between partners. In the lesson on establishing communities on other planets discussed earlier (in Excerpt 2), Mrs Larson asked the children to discuss in small groups what would be needed. Surjeet was in a small group with three boys: Sam and Jason who used only English at home with their families and Ricardo who spoke Tagalog at home. Mrs Larson was present at the beginning of their conversation:

(10)

Mrs L:	Is a dog essential?
Child:	It's an air.
Mrs L:	Is it something you absolutely have to have?
Children:	NO!
Child:	We need air.
Mrs L:	No, but what do you absolutely have to have?
Jason, Sam, Ricardo:	Air, air, air.
Surjeet:	Air.
Mrs L:	Yes, you need air. What else do you absolutely have to have? *Surjeet looking thoughtful, says 'eh:::'. Mrs Larson walks away* .
Ricardo:	Food! food! *(claps his hands)*
Surjeet:	*(looks at Ricardo)* Food! *(bounces as she says it, then stands up and looks at what Jason is writing)* Food. Drink. Drink.
Jason:	Food's the same as drink, Surjeet.
Surjeet:	Okay.
Sam:	*(to Jason)* No! You just keep printing it down there.
Jason:	Sorry I'm gonna do it on this.
Ricardo:	Yeah, don't just **. Drink! Drink!
Jason:	*(looks at Ricardo)* Drink is the same as, oh yeah, drink! *(He writes it down)*.
Surjeet:	Put drink there. No, put food with drink, eh? Nahh.
Jason:	Nah.
Surjeet:	Nah.
Jason:	D-r-ink *(sounding out)*
Surjeet:	ink, ink *(offering the final syllable)*
Jason:	No. <u>Drink</u>.
Surjeet:	Drink
Ricardo:	Drink-ing. Drinking?
Surjeet:	Drinking.
Jason:	Okay what else?

Surjeet's participation in this conversation was minimal, but complex. Her initial contribution was repeating 'air' after the other children. Later, she suggested that they need 'drink', but Jason rather witheringly told her that 'Food's the same as drink', a point with which she acquiesced. Several turns later, Ricardo told Jason that drink should be separate and Jason started to writes it down. Surjeet's 'Put drink there. No, put food with drink. Nahh' shows some of the internal contradictions sometimes evident in Surjeet's speech. I think she was initially echoing Ricardo's 'drink', then recalled Jason's point that 'food is the same as drink', then noticed that Jason was writing 'drink' down, so she contradicted her assertion with 'nahh'.

Throughout the rest of the interaction, she echoed the boys' statements, except in the following:

(11)

Sam:	Water!, water, water, water!
Jason:	Of course you need water *(starts to write it)*
Surjeet:	Drink
Sam:	Drink
Jason:	No, drink is water *(stops writing)*
Surjeet:	Yeah
Ricardo:	I got it! We need a, like when we, Mrs Larson showed that.
Sam:	Shelter.
Ricardo:	Yeah.
Jason:	What's shelter?
Surjeet:	Shelter.

While interpretation is difficult here, it appears that Surjeet was the first to remember that water might already be covered with 'drink', but one has the sense that her interlocutors did not credit her with detecting the possible error. Her later turns again echoed the boys' utterances.

Physically as well as linguistically, Surjeet was placed subordinately less centrally than the other children in the group and her placement affected her participation. The boys were sitting at three desks clustered together and Surjeet stood at her desk leaning over toward the boys. She was, of all the children, furthest from Jason and the worksheet. Eye contact between the boys was maintained throughout most of the conversation, with very little gaze toward Surjeet on anyone's part.

Surjeet's difficulties with being seen as a speaker who is 'understood ... believed, obeyed, respected, distinguished' are evident here (Bourdieu, 1977: 650) as they were in the previous grades. As the interaction proceeded, she continued to echo utterances of the boys, attempting (I think) to be a participant in the group work.

STUDENT-MANAGED CONVERSATIONS

Background

Much interesting work from a sociolinguistic perspective has examined how children manage their own conversations with one another (e.g. Corsaro & Rizzo, 1990; Goodwin, 1990). In this classroom, these sorts of conversations occurred at a variety of times. During Language Arts lessons, they occurred while students were completing written exercises at their desks, when they were preparing to start an activity, or at other transition points in the class. These conversations typically did not involve the lesson's topics. They showed similarities with the kindergarten 'colouring conversations' discussed in Excerpts 7, 16 and 18 in Chapter 2. I examine several of these conversations here and make observations about the purpose, positionality and meaning-creation aspects of the practice.

Student-managed conversations and the focal children

The following conversation occurred as children were colouring pictures near the end of the year, in June. Student-managed conversations in Language Arts lessons toward the end of their Grade 2 year were relatively infrequent, and notably quiet, with many children whispering; recording them became difficult. Throughout most of this lesson, Mrs Larson had monitored fairly closely the children's written completion of 'goal' statements for June. Some children had finished the activity and Mrs Larson was occupied speaking to individual children about their task completion. Sitting at one pod of tables were Julie, Amy, Leo and Jason:

(12)

Amy:	*(whispering)* Hey, Jason, guess which one is orange? *(holding up some felt crayons with the bottoms shielded by her hand)*
Jason:	Orange?
Amy:	Yeah.
Jason:	Yellow.
Amy:	This one is yellow, is yellow.
	(She shows the felts to Julie and Jason and giggles. She rearranges her seating, gets out another felt crayon and starts to colour again.)
	(Pause 15 seconds)[5]
	(To Jason concerning a crayon he is using.) Hey, that's Donald's.
Jason:	I know.
	Julie is very focused on her colouring, head bent over her paper, intent. Amy getting stuff out of her desk.
	(Pause 38 seconds)
Amy:	*(to Jason)* Does it smells, does it smells? Does it? How rude! *(looking in her supply box)*
	(Pause 7 seconds)
	Oh man, this is messy.
	Leo holds up some felts, covering part of them with his hand, like Amy did.
Leo:	Which one is, which one is blue?
Amy:	It's easy! You don't
	Jason reaches over and takes one.
Amy:	No:::!
	Jason holds up a blue one.
Amy:	Oh yeah, oh yeah.
Leo:	Come on.

Amy:	Okay, *(laughs)* my turn, my turn, my turn. *(She continues colouring.)*
	Julie is watching. She looks at classmates with wide eyes for a few seconds and then continues with her work.
Amy:	*(To someone out of frame, big intake of breath)* Hu::: You're in big trouble.

Amy apparently led this conversation, at least at its beginning, addressing Jason and showing her felts to Julie and Jason. Then Leo addressed her, continuing the guessing game she had started. The conversation was verbal, but also non-verbal; 'showing the felts' apparently made up part of the conversation. The conversation appeared desultory, as if Amy wished mainly to 'talk to talk' and to keep up some connection among the children at the table. The talk was relatively cooperative, with children responding to one another and not engaging in any obvious attempts to subordinate one another (except for Amy's 'It's easy!', which could have been a mildly scornful comment on Leo's attempt to play the guess-the-marker-colour).

Other positional efforts in student-managed conversations were not quite so benign. Student-managed conversations commonly included attempts to subordinate or degrade, as in the following:

(13)

Surjeet:	Look! Two more pages *(She shows her notebook to Jean Paul)*
Earl:	So what?
Jean Paul:	I don't care.
Earl:	Yeah, we don't care.
Jean Paul:	We've got two pages too. Look!
Surjeet:	No, three.
Jean Paul:	*(Aggressive tone, stands up to look at Surjeet's)* Oh! There's not three.
Earl:	I've got one page.
Jean Paul:	Let's see.
Surjeet:	You're m::: *(To Earl.)*
	She watches as Jean Paul inspects Earl's book.
Mrs L:	*(Calling across the room)* Jean Paul. Have you written out your goal yet?

Earl and Jean Paul dismissed Surjeet's initiating gambit, 'Look! Two more pages' as unworthy of attention. Earl attempted to 'one up' her by pointing out that he has even fewer pages left. Whatever Surjeet meant to say in her last turn, she cut herself off.

The next example highlights how meanings are created in student-managed conversations. Martin, Monique, Daisy and Earl were seated at the same pod of desks, cutting out paper stars on which to write their goals for the coming month.

(14)

Monique:	*(sneezes)* Oh, I was, I have, I have the sneezies.
Martin:	*** *(Colouring)*
Monique:	I'm allergic to dust mites. *(Gets up and goes out of frame)*
	Pause 12 seconds.
Martin:	*(To whom he is speaking is not clear. Daisy and Earl are possible, but he isn't looking at them.)*
	Nobody would be allergic to water, because water is everywhere. Water is in you. If somebody would be allergic to water, he wouldn't even be born. And someone would be allergic when he's a grown up, he would squeeze in him.
	Monique comes back to her desk.
	And if not, if you're allergic to water and you're grown up, people would be squeezing all your water out of your body.
Monique:	No, I'm allergic to dust mites.
Martin:	Well you know what? Water's everywhere. Even in you. *(leans forward)*
Monique:	No, <u>dust mites</u>!
Martin:	I know, but if you were allergic to water, you know how, what would happen?
Monique:	What?
Martin:	You wouldn't even get born.
Monique:	Why?
Martin:	That what happens. Water's everywhere –
Monique:	I sneeze all the time. Achoo, achoo, achoo. Just like
Martin:	And if you sneezed out, and then you sneezed on this *(gestures to his picture)* 'Achoo! I ruined it!' *(holds his head in mock horror)* 'It's all sneezie!'
Mrs L:	*(calling out to class)* Now, these people have still not given me their June goals. Listen for your name. Martin. I've asked you to cut it out. That's what you should be doing.
	Martin takes his scissors out of his desk and starts cutting.
	Anthony. Amy. Same to you. Monique. Cut it out now.
Monique:	*(to herself, irritated)* All right!
Mrs L:	Mary. And Jean Paul you're in line. Agatha. And Daisy. Please bring them up to me. Get them cut out and bring them up. Whether you're finished your colouring or not.
Monique:	*(is cutting out her star now)* If there's dust mites, probably I'll sniff and sneeze, 'cause I'm allergic to them. I am.
Martin:	Oh, I'm allergic to nothing.
Daisy:	I'm allergic to nothing.
Martin:	I'll become allergic to something soon.

Daisy: Yeah, me too.

Martin finishes cutting his star out and writes something on it, very focused.

In this excerpt, Martin, Monique and Daisy 'passed the time', expressed position and thought and talked about allergies, sneezing, dust mites and water. They struggled for topic control ('No, <u>dust mites</u>!'), speculated and reasoned. The conversation looked cooperative, collaborative and pleasurable. Although Martin held the floor more than the girls did, meaning was accomplished with them. The speakers contributed to a communicative chain. Each 'appropriates . . . word[s], adapting [them] to [their] own semantic and expressive intention' (Bakhtin, 1981: 293–4).

DISCUSSION

This discussion of the three classroom discourse practices analyzes them in terms of their purposes, the positional possibilities they offer to interactants, and finally, the possibilities they offer to interactants to construct voices and create meaning. The overlap between these aspects will be evident throughout discussion of all the discourse practices, so isolation of each is arbitrary for analytic purposes. I use these three perspectives to discuss views found in the literature as well as the data from my study.

Recitation sequences

Wells (1993) discussed the plurality of purposes for recitation sequences, presenting classroom data in which the teacher intended for the children to recall, create, exchange and/or extend information or knowledge. Wells' transcriptions show these goals being accomplished. Hall (1998) reported on her investigation of a secondary school classroom in which the teacher used the pattern (Hall's 'IRF': initiation, response, feedback) with the purpose of providing opportunities for second language students to speak and practise the second language. In Hall's data, the teacher frequently asked students questions about information they had which the teacher didn't (personal preferences, activities and so on); this practice allowed at least some students extended speaking opportunities. Mrs Larson pointed out another teacher purpose for the recitation sequence in her discussion of nominating Surjeet: to build confidence in children as learners, while allowing them to display their knowledge.

There are other views of latent or unintended purposes of recitation sequences. Wertsch (1998: 123), for example, claimed that recitation sequences involve teachers asking 'test questions' (questions to which they already know the answer) and that these test questions are 'creating and maintaining the relations of power and authority in classrooms'. Gutierrez and Larson (1994), using critical pedagogical and sociocultural theory, saw the practice as serving what they called hegemonic functions (preserving teacher power to control who speaks, about what and under what conditions). Wertsch argued that sociocultural practices mutually reinforce each other, and that practices such as the customary arrangement of speech acts in classrooms are congruent with desired social arrangements in other arenas.[6] Thus, maintaining the teacher as the locus of power and authority in classrooms appropriately and adaptively fits a system of which a central practice is ranking children on the basis of their performance on tests. Having individual children display their 'individually owned pieces of knowledge' before others congruently suits a philosophy of individual development and functioning (see Chapters 3 and 4). From this perspective, recalling, creating, exchanging or extending information or knowledge between students and teachers plays a less salient role in recitations than does creating and maintaining power positions for classroom participants.

Mrs Larson's purposes for recitation sequences seemed relatively uniform – in most cases, she used the recitation sequence to have children recall information that she believed the class had already discussed, or that the students knew (or should know). Her recitation sequences generally concern students supplying information she already had; her questions thus aimed to check whether or not individual children had this information.

Some researchers have seen the social relations that recitation sequences create and maintain as their primary purpose. This discourse pattern functions effectively to create and maintain the teacher as the originator, protector and manager of classroom knowledge and make children subordinate to the teacher in this regard. When teachers ask test questions, their position in terms of knowing is securely dominant.

Although teacher dominance in recitation sequences has been discussed frequently (e.g. Edwards & Westgate, 1994; Gutierrez & Larson, 1994; Wertsch, 1998), few analyses have examined in detail the concomitant subordination of students. My data illustrate some aspects of how students were subordinated in recitation sequences, in particular, individual students. McDermott (1993) showed graphically how some schooling activities are organised so as to define some participants as more able and some as less so; in his terms, they organise the search for differential performance, providing degradation possibilities. Recitation sequences belong to this class of activities. In Excerpt 2, for example, Surjeet's failure to supply the answer Mrs Larson expected was clearly apparent to everyone. The particular characteristics of this practice made Surjeet's failure salient not only to her teacher but also to other children, who witnessed her 'degradation'. Differential performance in recitation sequences allows differentiation of children and positions them in more or less desirable positions in their community. One of the larger consequences of Surjeet's commonly 'flawed' participation in recitation sequences was her teacher's evaluation of her as slow, unwilling to take risks and sometimes 'lazy'. Her failure to supply expeditiously the items needed to move the discourse along constructed her as occupying a flawed and undesirable identity position.

This matter of 'expeditious supplying' brings up another possibility for flaws in recitation performance. The preferred pacing of recitation sequences allows only minimal silences between teacher questions and student responses. Beginning teachers are sometimes advised to allow children longer than ordinary conversation 'wait time' to allow them the opportunity to organise responses. However, extraordinary[7] 'wait time' violates classroom verbal interaction norms. Teachers are not usually seen as the perpetrators of norm violations in this regard; rather, individual children are. Hence, not only can children be differentiated on the basis of their failure to supply 'right answers'; if they do not answer teacher questions at the 'right time', their performances can be judged as flawed.

Many commentators have maintained that the teacher's centrality in recitation sequences reduces opportunities for students to participate in the creation of divergent meanings (e.g. Gutierrez *et al.*, 1995; Nystrand *et al.*, 1997). In an analysis of one child's language in and out of school Tootoosis observed:

> On the whole, Leiha's language and that of her classmates in the context of the teacher-to-whole-class lesson format was limited in quantity, substance and purpose. The only purpose their language appeared to have was to demonstrate 'knowledge' by performing fill-in-the-blank and lead-in patterns for the teacher. There was no observed discovery, clarification or reworking of meaning. (Tootoosis, 1983: 155)

Surjeet was often silent when called upon by her teacher and her verbal contributions were slight and very quiet. The recitation pattern did not permit her a desirable place for legitimate peripheral participation, but rather functioned to show her as unable and subordinated. Martin rarely contributed to recitation sequences; he seldom volunteered for them, and the teacher nominated him infrequently as well. The verbal inventiveness and risk-taking with language he had displayed in kindergarten were not evident in his recitation sequence performances. Amy and Julie more frequently participated in recitation sequences; however, the form of student participation the sequence permitted meant that their contributions were never lengthy nor demonstrably useful for appropriating classroom language. Although Wells (1993) and Hall (1998) had found some contradictory enactments of recitation sequences, the practice constrained the focal children in terms of developing 'voice'.

Recitation sequences in this Grade 2 classroom presented few possibilities for the minority language focal children to engage in extended performance of language (cf. Cazden, 1988; Edwards & Westgate, 1994). Rather, these sequences affirmed the teacher's right to make classroom meaning, becoming one of many school practices that provided this affirmation. They thus exposed children to a dominant participation practice of school, linked to many other aspects of school social organisation, and gave them practice with contributing to teacher meanings. Although children could contribute to teacher meanings, they could not easily construct meanings (or voices) of their own in this practice. Although the teacher might have intended many of the recitation sequences to offer children the possibility of creating, exchanging and extending information and knowledge, the practice offered children little opportunity to construct extended utterances; their brevity meant that students got very little practice actually speaking English. As others have observed, the meanings expressed in the responses of recitation are teacher meanings, not child meanings; and participation seems primarily a matter of guessing teacher meanings.

Teacher-mandated peer conversations

Usually, educators recommend small group and partner conversations to give children opportunities for meaning making that rarely arise in large group discussions. Teachers intend that small group or partner conversations allow children to take longer and more frequent turns at talk than they might in large group formats, to ask as well as answer questions, to learn from peers, to make errors with reduced risk, and to rehearse for later performances.

Mrs Larson had two types of purposes for these small group and partner conversations. Sometimes she intended the children to complete relatively 'closed' tasks – completion of a worksheet, or of a group picture, or compilation of a group list. Sometimes the tasks appeared more 'open'; she asked children to speculate about personal meanings, about possible endings to stories, motives of characters and so on. The focal children's participation in the practice seemed to vary depending on whether the task was open or closed.

Advocates for peer conversations in classrooms have often remarked how, when children are grouped together without a teacher, their equal status relations as students promote their participation in a risk-free environment. In the Grade 2 classroom, sometimes the children did seem to be in partnerships or groups in which they negotiated relatively equal relations with their interlocutors (for example, Mary and Amy in Excerpt 7 and Martin and Jean-Paul in Excerpt 8). When children were friendly with one another, they seemed able to participate fully.[8] However, such horizontal positioning did not always characterise peer conversations; sometimes power relations were not horizontal (for example, among a group of boys and Surjeet in Excerpt 10, and between Amy and Julie in Excerpt 9). The children's positions in the interaction of course affected their participation. Citing Holland (1992), Eisenhart comments:

> Resistance, avoidance and lack of interest – when newcomers do not 'have their hearts in it' or, in other words, when they do not identify themselves as agents or actors in a cultural or social system – are associated with strikingly less expertise. (Eisenhart, 1995: 21)

In my data, when children could participate actively, and when they saw themselves as participants in the tasks mandated by the teacher, they did 'have their hearts in it', as when Martin and Jean Paul were storytellers (Excerpt 8). However, when the task was not one in which they could not actively participate or when the place they occupied was not pleasurable or desirable, the children, obviously alienated, did not appropriate classroom language nor did they attempt to express their own meanings.

When Mrs Larson gave the children a relatively open oral assignment like 'Tell your partner what you think might happen in this story', the children obviously had a great deal of fun composing story lines. In the *Ming Lo Moves the Mountain* lesson (Excerpts 7 and 8), Mrs Larson's questions were more or less open throughout the lesson: she asked children to 'Tell what might happen in this story', 'Tell what has happened in the story so far' , 'Tell what might happen next' and finally 'Tell what has happened in this story'. In cases where children could perform the mandated task (or when they transformed it into something they could do), partner and small group conversations obviously engaged children and led them to express vividly their own meanings. Jean Paul's and Martin's affirmation of themselves as storytellers appeared important in terms of maintaining them as legitimate peripheral participants in this activity (Excerpt 8).

When the tasks were less open, and when variant meanings seemed less welcome, the children evidenced less engagement. When the students had to interview one another about their food preferences within 'Canada's Food Groups', and fill in their findings on a photocopied worksheet, the worksheet and its implicit interview script took on authoritative presence in the conversation. The children interviewed one another with a script that discouraged their attempts to make their own meanings (Excerpt 9, for example, when Julie spurned Amy's swallowing your teeth foray). In cases when one child was the 'recorder' and had the piece of paper to write the answers to group work, to the extent that other children were distant from the paper, to that extent they appeared less central to the activity.

Surjeet's participation in peer conversations mandated by the teacher was difficult at times, especially under the circumstances of working in a small group with children with whom she did not have friendly relations otherwise. However, the practice 'freed' her voice in some ways; she participated more actively than she did in recitation sequences, although her participation often consisted of repetition of what other children had said (Excerpt 10). In light of the importance of verbal copying (see Chapter 4), this kind of participation appears as an initial stage in coming to voice in a setting. Martin's participation in small group conversations was usually enthusiastic and verbally inventive; he sometimes transformed the mandated tasks into tasks in which he was interested (Excerpt 8). Amy's participation in teacher-mandated small group and partner tasks illustrated a number of matters with regard to positionality. In some of these conversations, Amy actively participated and interacted with more experienced speakers of English so as to facilitate her appropriating a place in the conversation. However, in the 'food groups' conversation with Julie (Excerpt 9), Amy seemed somewhat subdued by the demands of the practice: although Amy wanted to speculate and comment beyond the sheet and beyond the task, Julie enforced the question, answer, question sequence which the worksheet set up. Julie's compliance with the task conventions prevented, rather than facilitated, her own and Amy's possibilities for using the conversation to go further. In other small group and partner conversations, dealing with stringently mandated tasks, children similarly took on (ventriloquated) the 'voice' of the teacher, acting as 'initiator' and 'evaluator'; other children acted as responders (or non-responders). Despite their status equality as children, and the fact that mistakes here did not matter much, the children would not stray very far from the task set for them. Conversely, when they were able to speculate, the children obviously found small group and partner conversations very engaging; they could express their own meanings and participate in collaborative meaning-making with peers.

Peer-managed conversations

Child-managed conversations in Grade 2, as in previous grades, showed patterns that differed considerably from conversations mandated by teachers for instrumental purposes. Although the teacher might intend recitation sequences and teacher-mandated conversations to create, exchange and extend information and knowledge, children's conversations more commonly served 'phatic' purposes: communication for the purpose of maintaining connections, for the sake of things being said, as well as for creating and exchanging information and knowledge. Hymes (1972: 40) noted that anthropologists Malinowski and Sapir had observed that phatic communication, 'talk for the sake of something being said . . . is far from a universally important or even acceptable motive' for conversations. In classrooms, teachers certainly sometimes see this motive as illegitimate. However, in many classrooms, teachers allow conversations for phatic purposes at certain times. Children obviously view talking-to-talk as an acceptable, common motive.

Some authors have assumed that there is status equality among children. However, the Grade 2 children's conversations obviously include attempts to position speakers and hearers, and attempts to position oneself and others. The sociopolitical function of each utterance in student conversations was not always apparent; it was much easier to take conversations, or at least exchanges, as the unit of analysis. I suspect that my occasional difficulties in understanding positionality at the utterance level had to do with my only part-time presence in the children's community. I think insiders can do utterance-level sociopolitical discursive analysis, but outsiders lack the requisite depth and historicity of understanding of the community's knowledge, except occasionally and serendipitously, to understand each utterance sociopolitically.

Sometimes the children's positioning did not appear obvious or hurtful, or the children could counter subordination attempts and maintain relations of (continually-negotiated) equality with other speakers in ways that allowed each to contribute meaningfully to the conversations (Martin and Monique in Excerpt 14). In other cases, children crudely expressed positioning and subordinated members could not counter their subordination. Throughout the years of research, the other children frequently dismissed and subordinated Surjeet. However, such behaviour not uncommonly occurs in children's conversations generally (Goodwin, 1990). Lensmire noted this same concern in his examination of the 'carnivalesque' aspects of writing workshops:

> There is an underside to children's relations that workshop advocates have not confronted. As in carnival, workshop participants sometimes use the free and playful space not to work out humane new relations, not to lampoon and discredit an unjust official order, but to reassert and reinforce ugly aspects of exactly that same unjust, larger society. Abuse in carnival (and the writing workshop) is not, as Bakhtin wanted it to be, solely aimed at worthy objects of uncrowning. Some targets are chosen because they are easy targets, because already uncrowned, never crowned. (Lensmire, 1996: 135)

Children engage in positioning themselves and their peers, not only in conversations where teachers are involved, but also in conversations among themselves. Helping children find desirable and powerful places in classroom activities requires attention to political as well as linguistic aspects of classroom interactions.

CONCLUSION

Bakhtin's distinction between authoritative and internally persuasive discourse helps understand some of the interactions in these Grade 2 Language Arts lessons. In authoritative discourse, someone assumes a position of authority over other speakers and allows other speakers no opportunity to 'play' in the text: 'the words of a father, of adults, of teachers, etc.' Bakhtin observes:

> Authoritative discourse permits no play with its borders, no gradual and flexible transitions, no spontaneously creative stylising variants on it . . . It is indissolubly fused with its authority – with political power, an institution, a person – and it stands and falls together with that authority. (Bakhtin, 1981: 343)

In contrast to this kind of discourse, Bakhtin poses the possibility of 'internally persuasive discourse', which is open to the 'interanimation' of other voices:

> Its creativity and productiveness consist precisely in the fact that such a word awakens new and independent words, that it organises masses of our words from within . . . The semantic structure of an internally persuasive discourse is not *finite*, it is *open*; in each of the new contexts that dialogise it, this discourse is able to reveal ever new *ways to mean*. (Bakhtin, 1981: 345–6, his italics)

The notion of internally persuasive discourse encourages the image of speakers engaging in a kind of mutual zone of proximal development, where participants have access to the expertise of others, the words of others, so that they are able to function 'as if they were a head taller than themselves' (Vygotsky, 1978: 102).

The classroom speech situations that eased the focal children's 'appropriation of words', were situations in which there was play with the borders, and where children could find 'ever new ways to mean'. When children could find desirable identities in words, play in words, when those words allowed them to 'answer back', and when the words of their community were open and accessible to them, then they transformed their participation, 'developing a range of voices . . . within and through [their] social identities in the many and varied interactive practices through which [they live] their lives.' (Hall, 1995).

Notes

1. Many teachers of my acquaintance claim that recitation sequences are much less common now than in the past. However, many contemporary researchers (Gutierrez & Larson, 1994; Johnson, 1995; Lemke, 1990; Nystrand *et al.*, 1997; Wertsch, 1998) are impressed by the extent to which they continue as major practices in classrooms. In the classrooms with which these researchers are familiar, as in the classrooms which I have observed, this sequence persists, although perhaps less frequently than before.

2. Mrs Larson remarked that she had been concerned since early in the year that Surjeet see herself as an able student; so, she deliberately asked Surjeet 'easy' questions. Believing that Surjeet often knew the answers to such, Mrs Larson made efforts to give her every opportunity to display her knowledge.

3. Baker (1997) discussed the complexity in transcription of assigning silences to speakers, making the point that attribution of silence constructs implications about character and competence. In this questioning routine in this class, I am confident that interactants understood the pauses in such interactions as being the student's silence.

4. 'Egg Waffles' is the name of a frozen prepared food available in local grocery stores. Capitalization in this transcript introduces a way of understanding this exchange not apparent without the capitalization. Baker (1997) and Roberts (1997) provide discussion of issues of importance in transcription.

5. One of the interesting aspects of student-managed conversations as shown above is that silence in them doesn't 'belong' to anyone, unlike in recitation sequences or even in teacher-mandated conversations. There are long silences in the conversation above, but I think it is clear that no one is responsible for filling this silence, and no one is liable to degradation on this basis. Much more than in recitation sequences and in mandated conversations, participation looks to be a matter of personal choice. One should probably not overstate this matter of personal choice, however. Julie does not verbally participate in this conversation, but apparently listens. In view of Mrs Larson's frequent reminders to the children to be quiet and stay focused on their task, Julie's silence here may be understood as not precisely her choice, but as compliance with a teacher directive. Amy's initiations, from this perspective, might be understood as resistance of a sort.

6. In a contribution to the email list, xmca, White (1998) observed:

    How about recognizing that within the system of systems of systems that teachers are actually doing what the system wants them to be doing? It is not enough to pathologize the teacher as the deliverer of school failure, and to fail to recognize that schools are supposed to fail students.

7. This observation, of course, begs the question, how long is extraordinary? I think that classrooms probably develop rhythms of their own, so that short and long wait times are defined situationally. It is thus impossible to quantify this except in relation to a particular classroom.

8. McDermott (1993) wrote that Adam performed well in those 'gentle circumstances of having a friend work with him'. When Amy and Mary worked together, for example, Mary's customary 'petting' of Amy extended to friendly collaboration around the task. On the other hand, when Surjeet was put in a group with boys with whom I had never observed her having playful relations, she appeared subordinated. This is not a particularly subtle observation: Most of us can articulate the experience of being more or less eloquent, funny, persuasive and so on depending (among other factors) on the social relations with our interlocutors.

CHAPTER 6

Appropriating Voices and Telling Stories

Language is not a neutral medium that passes freely and easily into the private property of the speaker's intentions; it is populated – overpopulated – with the intentions of others. Expropriating it, forcing it to submit to one's own intentions and accents, is a difficult and complicated process. (Bakhtin, 1981: 294)

Language is not a neutral medium; it comes to us loaded with social structure. It comes to us loaded with sensitivities to the circumstances under which it was born and maintained in previous encounters. It comes to us biased with the social agendas of a school system that pits all children against all children in a battle for school success. (McDermott, 1993: 293)

Schools have never been neutral places. For centuries schools have been places where some people's children learn to be subordinate to other people's children. (Grumet, 1988: 181)

I have described three years in the life of this group of school children from minority language backgrounds, viewing the children's engagements in the practices of their classrooms as filtered through a primary concern for how these children were learning English. In the discussion of the kindergarten year, I examined how school identity practices worked together to construct each child as a particular kind of student. With respect to the Grade 1 classroom, I noted physical, intellectual and linguistic practices that dislocated children one from another. These practices individualised the children and affected each focal child differently as the identity practices of kindergarten continued. In the Grade 2 classroom, I noted how the organisation of oral practices sometimes facilitated and sometimes blocked the focal children's access to opportunities for appropriating classroom language. I discussed the classroom data in terms of identity, resource distribution and discourse practices. These constructs provided variable but overlapping view of classroom events, to which I could then apply analytical perspectives derived from sociocultural theories, as opposed to the viewpoint traditional in SLA research.

IDENTITY, RESOURCE DISTRIBUTION AND DISCOURSE PRACTICES IN CLASSROOMS

In contrast to the view adopted in most SLA research, I have argued in this book that identity is not best regarded as an individual attribute or acquisition, but rather as the product of specific identity practices. The specific practices of their classrooms 'produced' the focal children as specific kinds of students, with the identity 'ESL learners' as a more or less important marker. They held the positions, not the internal essence, of being 'ESL' and 'quiet' or 'clever' or 'not so clever' and so on; these identities made sense only within the context of these particular practices. That identity practices are congruent with many other school practices, as well as with larger, societal ones should not lead to the supposition that they are natural or inevitable. As central practices, schools evaluate and rank children and thus manufacture identities for them.

In addition to identity practices, schools and classrooms (like other communities) have customary ways of distributing resources within them. I have argued that access to peers and their words and ideas are differentially distributed resources for children in classrooms that have major effects on their possibilities to participate in classroom activities, and thereby learn. Distribution of classroom resources are congruent, I argued, with practices in other arenas and, in this case, contributed to stratifying the classroom community on the 'natural' basis that some individuals had more in their heads (English, knowledge, numeracy, whatever).

Classrooms also organise particular ways for children and teachers to talk, read, write and listen, which differ from discursive practices in other communities. I examined oral discourse practices in lessons in a classroom with the objective of assessing how these practices had impacts on children's opportunities to appropriate classroom language and to create their own meanings. My research showed that children had most opportunities for appropriating classroom language in situations when they could speak from desirable and powerful identity positions, when they had access to the expertise of their peers, and when they could 'play' in language.

ACCESS TO VOICE

A variety of sociocultural theorists (Rogoff, 1990; Vygotsky, 1978; Wertsch, 1991) considering the sociality of instructional events and instructional 'mediations', have provided ways to think about language not so much as an isolated body of knowledge (and a goal in itself), but more as a tool that humans use to mediate their interactions (in McDermott's, 1993, terms, their 'conversations'). Obviously, this tool was – and sometimes remained – a resource differentially available to participants in the classroom communities I observed; they made differently successful attempts to grasp it.

Bakhtin's (1981, 1984, 1986) ideas about how learners come to participate in conversations, through appropriating the utterances of others, provided a means to examine how these novice users of English began to participate in classroom conversations. Bakhtin stressed that the appropriation of the words of others is a complex and conflictual process: because the historical, present and future positioning of speakers and those of their interlocutors are expressed in the 'very words' of utterances, words are not neutral but express particular cognitive predispositions, value systems and identity positions. Utterances, for Bakhtin, represent a voice, a perspective. Second language learning, then, becomes a struggle to come to voice. Learners must appropriate unfamiliar words and identity positions from others who may resist their appropriation – denying the legitimacy of 'those words' in 'those mouths'. Language learners face the complex and conflictual task of expressing their own meanings (suffused throughout with others' meanings) and finding responses for others' words.

Seeing speakers as members of specific social and historical collectivities moves observers toward examining the conditions for learning, for appropriation of practices, in any particular community. Contemporary sociocultural theorists (Lave & Wenger, 1991; Rogoff, 1990) have seen learning as a process of co-participation in community practices. From this perspective, educational research should focus not so much on trying to find out what individuals are doing 'beneath the skin and between the ears' (Mehan's, 1993: 241, apt phrase), but rather on the variety of positionings available for learners to occupy in their communities, social relations in particular communities, and the design and structure of the practices which bound the community. Conditions in different communities vary with regard to ease of access to expertise, to opportunities for practice, to consequences for error in practice and so on. All of these matters are important in analyzing how particular communities organise learning.

Lave and Wenger (1991) only point to the conflictual nature of social practice. Several other critical and poststructural theorists (Foucault, 1972, 1979; Gal, 1991; Hall, 1990; Taylor, 1989) have provided ways to discuss the nature of the identity positions and practices learners struggle to appropriate. In particular, Foucault discussed (1972, 1979) how discourse practices in contemporary Western cultures operate so that individuals are 'attached' to their own identities, positioned and categorised. He discussed practices for ranking individuals, as well as for normalising deviants. Children as well as adults create positionings through discourse practices; I discussed the effects of both children's and adults' efforts in this regard in terms of events in the classrooms I observed.

The classroom practices the children met in these three years provided differential opportunities for minority language background children to participate actively in classroom conversations and in so doing to appropriate voices in English. When children were legitimate peripheral participants in classroom activities, when the identities they occupied in those activities were desirable and powerful, and when they had access to their community's expertise, the children developed fuller roles in those activities. Sometimes children were prevented from full participation in these practices; the identities available to them were neither desirable nor powerful and their community's expertise was not available. Such situations correspondingly limited their opportunities for appropriation of school language as well as for appropriation of increasingly more active participation in other school activities.

FACILITATING ACCESS

This analysis implies that educators should attempt to find ways to build communities in which community resources are accessible to all, and in which desirable and powerful positions are available to all children. In the observed kindergarten classroom, imaginative play sometimes facilitated temporary construction of such communities and also facilitated minority language background children's appropriation of English voices. Choral work also permitted the children to be legitimate peripheral participants in activities, with little threat of degradation for inexperienced performance. Finding ways to encourage more of these kinds of activities in classrooms seems an important direction for further investigation.

Observations in the Grade 1 classroom centred around access to physical and intellectual resources of classrooms. This analysis suggested that attention to everyday matters like seating plans and permitted discursive contributions can provide useful information for easing children's opportunities to appropriate school language.

My observations in the Grade 2 classroom also give rise to some other simple recommendations for instructional practice for minority language background children: reduce recitation sequence time; increase peer conversation time; and explore ways to make partner and group work on the part of students more nearly collaborative than it sometimes is. Teachers will also face the challenge of trying to offset the subordination and domination efforts of students in conversations in which the teachers are not present.

Paley (1992) described a policy she developed in her classroom to block exclusion moves and suggested detailed steps to implement this policy. Researchers could also usefully investigate how to explicitly teach children to resist the subordination that seems omnipresent in their environments, so as to resist their exclusion from the conversations in which they need to be involved. Morgan (1997: 431) described work with adults in which the 'foregrounding of social power and identity issues . . . [lead to] . . . strategic resources for (re)defining social relationships', and which offers promise for some 'liberation' in children's classroom communities too. Norton Peirce (1995) described conversations with immigrant women in which aspects of power and identity were explicitly discussed and which appeared to lead to attempts on the women's part to resist subordination. These studies provocatively point out possible directions for work with children on resisting subordination and exclusion.

This work also implicitly challenges teachers to find new voices for themselves in classrooms. Students need teachers to scaffold their learning, to be more expert, to initiate them into new activities and communities of practitioners of those activities. Teachers can no doubt accomplish these charges by sometimes using authoritative voices (Bakhtin, 1981) with their students.

However, Bakhtin's work also highlights the need for teachers to struggle to appropriate voices for conversations with their students, to acquire points of view which allow teachers' and students' voices to interanimate one another's, to play with their borders and, to 'find ever newer ways to mean' together (Bakhtin, 1981: 345–6). Finding locally appropriate ways to structure such interaction is important future work.

INSTRUCTIONAL CONVERSATIONS

Some research on the discourse patterns in classrooms and their effects on minority language children has examined 'instructional conversations' (ICs) (Tharp & Gallimore, 1991). ICs are intended to engage students in classroom activities that facilitate their participation. In Goldenberg's (1991: 2) view: 'ICs are discussion-based lessons geared toward creating richly textured opportunities for students' conceptual and linguistic development'. Advocates of ICs see them displaying the following characteristics: (a) the teacher provides a thematic focus, (b) the teacher activates and elicits students' background knowledge, (c) the teacher provides direct teaching as necessary, (d) the teacher elicits extended student contributions through invitations to expand, questions, restatements and pauses, (e) the teacher gently probes to get students to support their arguments or positions, (f) the teacher asks questions for which there may be more than one correct answer, (g) the teacher responds to students' statements, (h) the teacher provides a challenging but non-threatening atmosphere, (i) participants self-select speaking turns.

Several descriptions of ICs (Goldenberg, 1991; Patthey-Chavez et al., 1995; Tharp & Gallimore, 1991) are available and their transcripts illustrate convincingly that such conversations look (sound) different in many ways from recitation scripts. The most salient apparent differences are the IC's self-selection of turns and provision of questions that have more than one correct answer. This interesting line of investigation of classroom practice intersects with work by Hall (1998) and Wells (1993), who showed conversations between students and teachers that appear to be recitation sequences, but which have very different outcomes from those noted in Chapter 5.[1] In the conversations Wells analyzed, the teacher extended students' answers, drew out their significance and made connections with other parts of the lesson. In addition, the topics of the episodes seemed to be co-constructed by both the teacher and the students. Hall (1998) showed IRF sequences that permitted at least some students extended opportunities to practise a second language.

Another promising line of investigation in this regard is that of Gutierrez *et al.* (1995: 467). They analyzed a classroom interaction characterised primarily by a teacher's 'script' and students' 'scripts of resistance'. They noted brief incidents (which they term, 'participation in a third space') in which neither teacher's nor the students' voices seem dominant and wherein dialogue occurs as 'various cultures, discourses and knowledges are made available to all classroom participants'.

It remains unclear with respect to ICs, the conversations Wells or Hall described, or the 'third space' conversations, whether some children, but not others, are privileged with respect to their participation. One cannot tell whether other children have differential difficulties finding desirable, powerful or even equal places in these conversations. These are questions for future research. However, this work has provided examples of classroom dialogues that appear richly promising.

THE POLITICS OF REPRESENTATION

This book offers representations of events and people, selections among the many events that I observed during the three years. I told individual stories about the focal children, using my observations and transcriptions of interactions to 'build up the case' for regarding the children in specific ways, and sometimes for contesting representations made of them by their teachers. As the cultural theorist S. Hall (1990: 222) remarked 'Practices of representation always implicate the positions from which we speak or write'. As a university researcher, I had the employment (and research grant) obligation to make sense of what I observed, to code that sense-making in written academic discourse, and to do so competently, credibly, persuasively and interestingly to academic colleagues and (I hoped) eventually to practising teachers. My discourse communities, my obligations to them, and the discourse (and other) activities in which I customarily and obligatorily engage differ from those of the teachers, parents and children in whose classrooms I observed.

Teachers also make representations of persons and events in their classrooms; they are obligated by virtue of their employment to do so. They make representations of their students orally in discussions with colleagues and parents. They are obligated to represent the children in writing on report cards for an audience of administrators, parents, future teachers of the children, and sometimes the children themselves. With the further legal obligations to maintain order and teach government-mandated curriculum in their classrooms, teachers' activities and discourse communities differ from those of researchers, parents and children; their representations of people and events likewise differ.

Parents and children also represent people and events in classrooms. Their perceptions, interpretive frameworks, modes of and audiences for reporting are different from those of researchers and teachers. Thus, what they see and what they say about what they see may well be very different from what other participants might see and say.

The feminist philosopher S. Bordo (1990) quoting Nietzsche (1969: 119), noted that seeing and knowing are always perspectival and never 'innocent':

> We always 'see' from points of view that are invested with our social, political and personal interests, inescapably 'centric' in one way or another, even in the desire to do justice to heterogeneity. (Bordo, 1990: 140)

Thus, aspects of identity affect the representations people create; aspects of the practices in which they engage also affect their representations. My various positions and practices as an observer, researcher, mother of elementary school-aged children, white middle-aged Canadian woman who went to Canadian schools, speaker of English, former teacher of children, and current university teacher, and so on are implicated in the ways I have represented this classroom and the persons therein. Contradictions between my perceptions of the identities of the children I observed, their parents' perceptions, their teachers' perceptions, their classmates' perceptions and the children's own perceptions would be logical, given our different positions not only within the classroom but also within the wider social networks in which we live.

However, acknowledging that there will be difference in differently positioned observers' representations may not be quite enough. As Mehan (1993) pointed out, representations have politics:

> Events in the world are ambiguous. We struggle to understand these events, to imbue them with meaning. The choice of a particular way of representing events gives them a particular meaning. There is often a competition over the correct, appropriate, or preferred way of representing objects, events or people. Competition over the meaning of ambiguous events, people and objects in the world has been called the 'politics of representation'. (Mehan, 1993: 241)

Mehan described the case of a child involved in a referral process for special education; the psychologist's view of the child became privileged over those of the child's mother and classroom teacher. Although the psychologist had the least historical and contextual knowledge of the child, the psychologist's view, a view with which the teacher and mother did not initially agree, prevailed. Mehan pointed out, 'The psychologist's language obtains its privileged status because it is ambiguous, because it is full of technical terms, because it is difficult to understand' (Mehan, 1993: 258). The psychologist's view is presented to others in a report; the mother's and the classroom teacher's views are elicited from them by questions.

In research, privilege with regard to representation is complex. Although writing a book might in some ways privilege my voice over those of the children, their teachers and parents, my version of events is not necessarily that which survives in the written documentation of the children's report cards, or in their memories, or in those of their teachers and parents.

Many researchers, concerned about the politics of representation in qualitative educational research, have advocated official collaboration between teachers and researchers (and sometimes, students) so that research would reflect more broadly all participants' perceptions and so that the researcher's voice, an outsider's, is de-centred. Such researchers hope that the presentation of multiple points of view, that may well contradict each other, will lead to increased understandings of particular events or sites. Although I am sympathetic to such views, I did not engage in collaboration with the children or the teachers in this study for the following reasons.

I began this exploratory study with the intention of observing in the classrooms in as non-obtrusive a manner as possible, more as a matter of tact with regard to the research site and its participants, and uncertainty with respect to what was (or should be) going on in the classrooms of young children, than as a deliberate methodological stance. As it happened, fieldnote recording occupied so much attention that occasional conversations in the classrooms with any particular child or group of children, meant missed opportunities to record other events or aspects of context not accessible to audio- or video-tape recording. This stance of relative non-engagement with the children allowed me to be quietly present in many of their interactions. Later, I worried that more actively pursuing conversations with the children in or out of school might negatively affect my observer status. My interest in seeing what the children did in their classrooms, whom they became and what they said as a result of those activities, also made me less interested in what they might say in outside-school interviews about school. I was also unsure of how best to approach interviewing young children like these. Hence, this account does not directly represent the children's voices in reflection on matters in their classroom or on what I observed.[2] However, the extensive and, insofar as practical, accurate (cf. Roberts, 1997) quotations of the children's voices while engaged in classroom activities ought to give other observers the data they might need to engage with and assess my interpretations. I present here as well sociological (at least with regard to their classrooms) and limited historical information about the children.

Neither did I engage in collaboration with the teachers in whose classrooms I was made so welcome. Having been a public school teacher, having taught in a variety of adult education agencies while completing my graduate studies, having two siblings who are public school teachers, and having taught teachers for a long time, I am aware that in many ways I perceive and act on the world from the perspective of teacher. I do not now teach children, but I am certainly a legitimate peripheral participant in a community of teachers. In this research, I wished to disrupt my usual affiliation so that I might primarily observe children, and not participate in a teacher discourse community about those children. Knowing that this would only partially succeed did not dissuade me. I wanted to develop analyses of activities in these classrooms as someone who saw them as 'artificial creations . . . organised around beliefs and practices that control and regulate the intellectual life of students' (Moll, 1992: 23). I believed that classroom practices would appear more salient to me, and that I could better maintain a position of speculation about them, if I occupied in some sense a 'newcomer' or 'outsider' position.

Despite not collaborating in depth with the teachers, I did interview them several times over the course of the study and incorporated their information, suggestions, speculations and explanations into this text. Mehan (1993) illustrates problems inherent in privileging the voice of the person with the most institutional status but the least experience with the children. To deal in some way with these problems, I presented drafts of the chapters that concerned them to the teachers involved and asked them to respond in whatever way suited them. Although some of my descriptions and analyses could be construed as critical of classroom practices, the teachers in whose classrooms observations were made, in every case met them with professional interest. One teacher said after reading the first draft of a paper, 'It's not at all how I would have described the classroom, but there's nothing in it that's inaccurate'. Another teacher vigorously disagreed with some aspects of my first attempts at analysis of practices in her classroom. The discussions I had with all the teachers about their perceptions of what I had written sharpened and clarified my writing, and provided some different perspectives (see, for example, Toohey, 1998). Although they still may not agree with everything I have written, they acknowledge the differences in our perspectives and have approved of my quotation of their voices here.

Bordo cautioned against the 'supposition that if we employ the right method', we can produce representations which can be 'politically correct'. As she put it:

> The dynamics of inclusion and exclusion . . . are played out on multiple and shifting fronts, and all ideas (no matter how 'liberatory' in some contexts or for some purposes) are condemned to be haunted by a voice from the margins, already speaking (or perhaps presently muted but awaiting the conditions for speech), awakening us to what has been excluded, effaced, damaged. (Bordo, 1990: 138)

I acknowledge that the methods employed in this study do not provide all the participants' voices with equal access to the 'floor'; some speak from the margins, some mutely wait. Foucault (1979) argued that it is naive to believe that there can be production of knowledge without differential power. Knowing that someone or some ideas would always be excluded, I decided in this case that it was worthwhile to try to examine classroom interactions without collaboration with other participants.

Many educational researchers have powerfully demonstrated teachers' contributions to enriching understandings of classroom events (Connelly & Clandinin, 1988; Jervis *et al.*, 1996; Nunan, 1992; and many others). However, Bell has observed a paucity of 'teacher research' in the field of second language learning. She argued that teachers' involvement in research in their classrooms would make this research more likely 'to improve our understanding of the field and eventually to influence practice' (Bell, 1997: 5). I am convinced of the importance of such discussion and am currently involved in such a project.

CONVERSATIONS, NOT COLLABORATIONS

Despite their necessity, conversations between teachers and researchers about what is going on in their classrooms are sensitive and complicated. Increasingly, as they report their collaborations with teachers, researchers describe disrupted relationships, 'betrayals' and a variety of difficulties (e.g. Evans, 1998; Moje, 1998). These conflicts arise because such conversations occur in particularly delicate circumstances.

All teachers have personal experience being students of university professors. Bakhtin described 'the words of a father, of adults, of teachers' as examples of authoritative texts. The words of university professors in university classrooms often take the form of authoritative text; in education classes, professors commonly offer opinions about preferred and non-preferred classroom practices, in effect, telling teachers what they should do. The positioning this sets up in university classrooms has effects on subsequent professor–teacher discussions.

In schools, however, teachers are the authorities, not professors or researchers. Conversations in schools between teachers and researchers about classroom practice become more or less confusing due to the contradictory relations of power. A researcher's critical remarks about a teacher's practices in a school research site (perhaps acceptable in university classrooms when the critiqued practices are hypothetical) might easily disrupt their relationship, which usually exists only at the teacher's sufferance. Researchers thus find it easier (and less dangerous) to maintain in such situations a friendly and non-challenging demeanour.

Finding ways to have respectful, productive and sometimes conflictual conversations with teachers about classroom practice in these circumstances is difficult; teachers as well as researchers must enter willingly into such conversations. Asking respectful but critical questions, reframing utterances, voicing disagreement dialogically, strategically self-disclosing and displaying commitment to further dialogue are elements of a 'social language' (cf. Bakhtin, 1981) which appears less well-known in schools and universities than it might be. However, I believe it is only in such discourse that teachers and researchers will affect one another's practice. Speaking about classroom events that might be construed as troubling or ambiguous, in ways that allow the continuation of the relationship, will involve both parties finding new ways to speak.

Bakhtin (1981) poses the possibility of 'internally persuasive discourse', which is open to the 'interanimation' of other voices, which allows participants to create 'ever newer ways to mean'. Learning ways of speaking about classroom practices which are authoritative, as well as open, playful and able to reveal ever new ways to mean, will perhaps involve developing new and unfamiliar teaching and research practices. These new practices will have to examine explicitly issues of power inherent in teacher–researcher relationships and issues of individual versus joint responsibility. Future work that explores these relationships and discourse practices will no doubt guide researchers to other necessary issues.

FUTURE SLA RESEARCH

I have argued here that the traditional SLA notion of language learning as individual internal processing of second language input and production of second language output has not suficiently examined the practices, activities and social contexts in which learners engage. I also argued that attention to these matters is important, not only because they are commonly overlooked in much SLA research, but also because the development of socially and pedagogically useful understandings of SLA must take into account the realities of learners' circumstances. Learners' investments in learning a second language (Norton Peirce, 1995; Norton, 2000), the ways in which their social identities and positioning affect their participation in second language conversations (Leung *et al.*, 1997; McKay & Wong, 1996; Morgan, 1997), their access to participation in the activities of their communities and the obstacles to participation they experience, must all be matters of consideration in future research.

At the same time that this newer research takes the social world of learners seriously into account, future SLA research will also need to develop complex understandings of how individual human learners understand their social worlds and their place(s) in them. Forman *et al.* (1993: 6) pointed out that an emphasis on the sociocultural contexts of human beings should not obscure from view 'real people who develop a variety of interpersonal relationships with one another in the course of their shared activity in a given institutional context'. Kirshner and Whitson (1997) argued that 'the notion of the individual in situated cognition theory needs to be fundamentally reformulated' so as to avoid reducing human experience to only the socially given. For them, this reformulation involves investigation of the 'physiological, psychoanalytic, and semiotic constitution of persons' and their collection includes studies which illustrate these approaches (Lave, 1997; Walkerdine, 1997). Litowitz (1997) discussed psychoanalytic and sociological work which emphasises the importance of intersubjectivity, resistance and identification in desires to learn and participate in certain activities. Day (1999) explored how a young English learner participated in a variety of communities of practice in his classroom and the affiliations and identifications he developed in these practices. All of these studies provide models of how this reformulation of ideas of individuals as embodied, semiotic and emotional persons, situated in communities, might be accomplished. Reformulation of language learning theory will require investigation and integration of these complex means of understanding learners and learning.

AFTERWORD

Finding appropriate genres for internally persuasive discourse about changing school practices has preoccupied many writers, who have worried that such writing often carries so many associations with previous authoritative discourse on this topic. Lee (1985), for example, used letters between a teacher and a researcher to open a conversation about how teachers can engage in anti-racist practices. Paley (1986, 1989, 1992, 1996) used narrative, speculation and direct quotations from the children in her kindergarten to explore a variety of educational issues. Although educational researchers struggle to find ever new ways to write about educational practices, I believe conversations that teachers have among themselves, as well as conversations between teachers and researchers, will in fact forge concrete ideas for changing classroom practices. The following is my contribution to those conversations, where I will not be physically present.

I have tried here to show that what school practices are determines who particular participants can be, what they can do, and thus what they can learn in that setting. For example, if the children I observed had been less commonly engaged in solo speech performance in front of their peers, their teacher's and peers' evaluations of their achievements might have been different. If accuracy of performance on 'concentration' memory games with cards, or intricacy and detail of drawings, or elaboration of construction of Lego structures, or sensitivity to peers and the teacher, were items for school evaluation, for example, the focal children's identities might have turned out somewhat differently. What is done in schools, and what is considered knowledge in schools, are socially and culturally specific; some children will be disadvantaged and others advantaged by the decisions made about these matters. Had practices been different in the classrooms in which they were enrolled, the focal children might have finished Grade 2 with identities other than those they had. Surjeet might have been seen as an enthusiastic writer, whose family was very supportive of and concerned with her educational progress, and her careful attention to many events in her classroom might have been seen as evidence of her learning capabilities. Martin might have been seen as a gifted young artist with formidable powers of concentration and dedication to finishing his projects: his attempts to examine his world creatively, his humour and his struggle to represent his experiences, despite his beginner status with respect to English, might have been matter for celebration. Harvey's structural skills with model building might have been noticed and cited as evidence of his potential as a learner. Julie's and Amy's strengths in their classroom might have been formulated as other than 'nice little girl'. These children might have been different, had school practices been different.

Changing school practices so as to provide all children with desirable and powerful positions in their classrooms is an objective most educators share. Recognising that more ethnic diversity in schools meant that classroom participants came with more diverse educational experiences, Hicks (1995: 86) argued that educational and teacher researchers might 'need to begin serious inquiry into how the heterogeneous voices of students and teachers situationally constitute classroom discourses and what counts as academic knowledge'. I have told stories here about these children in their classrooms in order to illuminate some of the complexities of classroom discourses and their effects on the children and their learning.

Virginia Woolf (1977: 123) provided a lyrical estimation of the worth of stories, writing ' . . . inconclusive stories are legitimate; that is to say, though they leave us feeling melancholy and perhaps uncertain, yet somehow or other they provide a resting point for the mind'. The stories I have told here about the children and their classrooms are inconclusive, but I hope they do provide resting (or in some cases, troubling) points for the mind. They begin with the children's entry into kinder-garten, and end at the end of the children's Grade 2 year. Two of the children have left Canada, Julie for Poland and Amy for Hong Kong, and they will not be schooled in English. Randy has moved to another school in Suburban City. The other chil-dren, Harvey, Martin and Surjeet, continue to attend Suburban School and continue to learn to use the English of their classrooms and community. I have written about my observations of these children during their first three years of school, hoping that my report of their participation in classroom activities might help other teachers and educators. Observing other children, they must consider classroom practices which might permit those children to participate in a variety of social milieux as speakers, to find voices from which to speak, and to find ways to develop different discourses. These will be both authoritative and internally persuasive: discourses that are some-times fused with authority, but are also sometimes, in Bakhtin's words, playful at the boundaries, half one's own, and half someone else's. I sincerely hope that I have presented these stories and my interpretations of them in ways that invite the answering words of others.

Notes

1. In analysis of a recitation script in a classroom in a Punjabi Sikh school, my colleagues and I have also seen some intriguing other possibilities for this script (Toohey *et al.*, 2000).
2. For this reason, speculation about the children's 'investments' (cf. Norton Peirce, 1995) in learning English was precluded, although some notions of their parents' investments were mentioned.

References

Agre, P. (1997) Living math: Lave and Walkerdine on the meaning of everyday arithmetic. In D. Kirshner and J.A. Whitson (eds) *Situated Cognition: Social, Semiotic and Psychological Perspectives*. Mahwah, NJ: Lawrence Erlbaum.

Appel, G. and Lantolf, J.P. (1994) Speaking as mediation: A study of L1 and L2 text recall tasks. *The Modern Language Journal* 78, 437–52.

Baker, C.D. (1997) Transcription and representation in literary research. In J. Flood, S.B. Heath and D. Lapp (eds) *Handbook of Research on Teaching Literacy through the Communicative and Visual Arts*. New York: Macmillan.

Bakhtin, M. (1981) *The Dialogic Imagination: Four Essays*. Austin, TX: University of Texas Press.

Bakhtin, M. (1984) *Esthétique de la Création Verbale*. Paris: Gallimard.

Bakhtin, M. (1986) *Speech Genres and other Late Essays* (trans.V.W. McGee). Austin, TX: University of Texas Press.

Bell, J. (1997) Teacher research in second and foreign language education. *The Canadian Modern Language Review* 54, 3–10.

Berk, L. and Winsler, A. (1995) *Scaffolding Children's Learning: Vygotsky and Early Childhood Education* (Vol. 7). Washington DC: National Association for the Education of Young Children.

Birdwhistell, R. (1970) *Kinesics and Context: Essays on Body Motion Communication*. Philadelphia: University of Pennsylvania Press.

Bordo, S. (1990) Feminism, post-modernism, and gender skepticism. In L. Nicholson (ed.) *Feminism/Postmodernism*. New York: Routledge.

Bourdieu, P. (1977) The economics of linguistic exchanges. *Social Science Information* 16, 645–668.

Bourdieu, P. (1984) *Distinction. A Social Critique of the Judgement of Taste* (trans. R. Nice). London: Routledge & Kegan Paul.

Bourne, J. (1992) Inside a multilingual primary classroom: A teacher, children and theories at work. Unpublished doctoral thesis, University of Southampton.

137

Brislin, R.W. (1981) *Cross Cultural Encounters: Face to Face Interaction*. New York: Pergamon Press.

Bryson, M. and de Castell, S. (1997) En/gendering equity: Paradoxical consequences of institutionalized equity policies. In S. de Castell and M. Bryson (eds) *Radical In<ter>Ventions: Identity, Politics and Differences in Educational Praxis*. Albany: SUNY Press.

Cazden, C. (1988) *Classroom Discourse: The Language of Teaching and Learning*. Portsmouth, NH: Heinemann.

Cazden, C. (1993) Vygotsky, Hymes and Bakhtin: From word to utterance and voice. In E. Forman, N. Minick and C.A. Stone (eds) *Contexts for Learning: Sociocultural Dynamics in Children's Development*. New York: Oxford University Press.

Cole, M. (1992) Culture in development. In M.H. Bornstein and M.E. Lamb (eds) *Developmental Psychology: An Advanced Textbook* (3rd edn). Hillsdale, NJ: Erlbaum.

Cole, M. (1996) *Cross-Cultural Psychology: A Once And Future Discipline*. Cambridge, MA: The Belknap Press of Harvard University Press.

Cole, M. (1998) Can cultural psychology help us think about diversity? Paper presented at the American Educational Research Association meetings, San Diego, CA.

Collins, J. (1993) Determination and contradiction: An appreciation of and critique of the work of Pierre Bourdieu on language and education. In C. Calhoun, E. Lipuma and M. Postone (eds) *Bourdieu: Critical Perspectives*. Chicago: University of Chicago Press.

Connelly, M. and Clandinin, J. (1988) *Teachers as Curriculum Planners: Narratives of Experience*. New York: Teachers College Press.

Corder, P. (1967) The significance of learners' errors. *International Review of Applied Linguistics* 5, 161–70.

Corsaro, D. and Rizzo, T. (1990) Disputes and conflict resolution among nursery school children in the U.S. and Italy. In A. Grimshaw (ed.) *Conflict Talk*. Cambridge: Cambridge University Press.

Dagenais, D. and Berron, C. (1998) Une étude ethnographique des pratiques langagières en famille immigrante. Paper presented at the Canadian Society for Studies in Education meetings, Ottawa, Ontario.

Davis, K. (1995) Qualitative theory and methods in applied linguistic research. *TESOL Quarterly* 29, 427–54.

Day, E. (1999) Identity formation in a kindergarten English second language learner: An ethnographic case study. Unpublished doctoral dissertation, Simon Fraser University.

Duff, P. and Uchida, Y. (1997) The negotiation of teachers' sociocultural identities and practices in postsecondary EFL classrooms. *TESOL Quarterly* 31, 451–86.

Dulay, H. and Burt, M. (1974) Natural sequences in child second language acquisition. *Language Learning* 24, 37–53.

Dulay, H. , Burt, M. and Krashen, S. (1982) *Language Two*. New York: Oxford University Press.

Duranti, A. and Goodwin, C. (eds) (1992) *Rethinking Context: Language as an Interactive Phenomenon*. Cambridge: Cambridge University Press.

Edwards, A.D. and Westgate, D.P.G. (1994) *Investigating Classroom Talk* (2nd edn). London: The Falmer Press.

Eisenhart, M. (1995) The Fax, the jazz player, and the self-story teller: How do people organize culture? *Anthropology and Education Quarterly* 26, 3–26.

Ellis, R. (1994) *The Study of Second Language Acquisition*. Oxford: Oxford University Press.

Ellis, R. (1998) Teaching and research: Options in grammar teaching. *TESOL Quarterly* 32, 39–60.

Ervin-Tripp, S. (1974) Is second language learning like the first? *TESOL Quarterly* 8, 111–27.

Evans, K.S. (1998) Negotiating roles in collaborative research: Re-examining issues of power and equity. Paper presented at the American Educational Research Association meetings, San Diego, CA.

Faltis, C. (1993) *Joinfostering: Adapting Teaching Strategies for the Multilingual Classroom*. New York: Maxwell Macmillan International.

Fine, M. (1985) Dropping out of high school: An inside look. *Social Policy*, Fall, 43–50.

Forman, E., Minick, N. and Stone, C.A. (1993) Introduction. In E. Forman, N. Minick and C.A. Stone (eds) *Contexts for Learning: Sociocultural Dynamics in Children's Development*. New York: Oxford University Press.

Foucault, M. (1972) *Power/Knowledge: Selected Interviews and Other Writings*. New York: Pantheon Books.

Foucault, M. (1979) *Discipline and Punish: The Birth of the Prison* (trans. A. Sheridan). New York: Vintage Books.

Freire, P. (1970) *Pedagogy of the Oppressed*. New York: Seabury Press.

Furnham, A. and Bochner, S. (1986) *Culture Shock: Psychological Reactions to Unfamiliar Environments*. London: Routledge.

Gal, S. (1991) Between speech and silence: The problematics of research on language and gender. In M. di Leonardo (ed.) *Gender at the Crossroads of Knowledge: Feminist Anthropology in the Postmodern Era*. Berkeley, CA: University of California Press.

Genesee, F. (1994) *Educating Second Language Children: The Whole Child, the Whole Curriculum, the Whole Community*. Cambridge: Cambridge University Press.

Gibbons, P. (1993) *Learning to Learn in a Second Language*. Portsmouth, NH: Heinemann.

Goffman, E. (1976) *Gender Advertisements*. New York: Harper & Row.

Goodman, Y. and Goodman, K. (1994) Vygotsky in a whole-language perspective. In L.C. Moll (ed.)*Vygotsky and Education: Instructional Implications and*

Applications of Sociohistorical Psychology. Cambridge: Cambridge University Press.

Goodwin, M.H. (1990) *He-Said-She-Said: Talk as Social Organization among Black Children*. Bloomington, IN: Indiana University Press.

Goldenberg, C. (1991) *Instructional Conversations and their Classroom Application*. Washington, DC: Office of Educational Research and Improvement.

Grumet, M. (1988) *Bitter Milk: Women and Teaching*. Amherst, MA: University of Massachusetts Press.

Gumperz, J. (1992) Contextualization and understanding. In A. Duranti and C. Goodwin (eds) *Rethinking Context: Language as an Interactive Phenomenon*. Cambridge: Cambridge University Press.

Gutierrez, K. and Larson, J. (1994) Language borders: Recitation as hegemonic discourse. *International Journal of Education* 31, 22–36.

Gutierrez, K., Rymes, B. and Larson, J. (1995) Script, counterscript, and underlife in the classroom: James Brown versus Brown v. Board of Education. *Harvard Educational Review* 65, 445–71.

Hakuta, K. (1974) A report on the development of grammatical morphemes in a Japanese girl learning English as a second language. *Working Papers on Bilingualism* 4, 18–44.

Hall, J.K. (1993) The role of oral practices in the accomplishment of our everyday lives: The sociocultural dimension of interaction with implications for the learning of another language. *Applied Linguistics* 14, 145–65.

Hall, J.K. (1995) (Re)creating our worlds with words: A sociohistorical perspective of face-to-face interaction. *Applied Linguistics* 16, 206–32.

Hall, J.K. (1998) Differential teacher attention to student utterances: The construction of different opportunities for learning in the IRF. *Linguistics and Education* 9, 287–311.

Hall, S. (1990) Cultural identity and diaspora. In J. Rutherford (ed.) *Identity: Community, Culture, Difference*. London: Lawrence and Wishart.

Hanks, W. (1991) Foreword. In J. Lave and E. Wenger (eds) *Situated Learning: Legitimate Peripheral Participation*. Cambridge: Cambridge University Press.

Hatch, E. (ed.) (1978) *Second Language Acquisition: A Book of Readings*. Rowley, MA: Newbury House.

Hazzard, S. (1970) *The Bay of Noon*. New York: Penguin.

Hicks, D. (1995) Discourse, learning and teaching. In M. Apple (ed.) *Review of Research in Education* 21. Itasca: F.E. Peacock.

Holland, D. (1992) How cultural systems become desire: A case study of American romance. In R. D'Andrade and C. Strauss (eds) *Human Motives and Cultural Models*. Cambridge: Cambridge University Press.

Huang, J. and Hatch, E. (1978) A Chinese child's acquisition of English. In E. Hatch (ed.) *Second Language Acquisition: A Book of Readings*. Rowley, MA: Newbury House.

Hull, G. and Rose, M. (1989) Rethinking remediation: Towards a social-cognitive understanding of problematic reading and writing. *Written Communication* 6, 139–54.

Hymes, D. (1972) Models of the interaction of language and social life. In J.J. Gumperz and D. Hymes (eds) *Directions in Sociolinguistics: The Ethnography of Communication*. New York: Holt Rinehart and Winston.

Itoh, H. and Hatch, E. (1978) Second language acquisition: A case study. In E. Hatch (ed.) *Second Language Acquisition: A Book of Readings*. Rowley, MA: Newbury House.

Jervis, K., Carr, E., Lockhart, P. and Rogers, J. (1996) Multiple entries to teacher inquiry: Dissolving the boundaries between research and teaching. In L. Baker, P. Afflerbach and D. Reinking (eds) *Developing Engaged Readers in School and Home Communities*. Mahwah, NJ: Lawrence Erlbaum.

Johnson, K.E. (1995) *Understanding Communication in Second Language Classrooms*. Cambridge: Cambridge University Press.

Kanno, Y. and Applebaum, S.D. (1995) ESL students speak up: Their stories of how we are doing. *TESL Canada Journal* 12, 32–49.

Kirshner, D. and Whitson, J.A. (eds) (1997) *Situated Cognition: Social, Semiotic and Psychological Perspectives*. Mahwah, NJ: Lawrence Erlbaum.

Klein, M.H., Alexander, A.A. and Tseng, K.-H. (1971) The foreign students adaptation program: Social experience of Asian students. *International Educational Cultural Exchange* 6, 77–90.

Kramsch, C. (1993) *Context and Culture in Language Teaching*. Oxford: Oxford University Press.

Kress, G. (1989) *Linguistic Processes in Sociocultural Practice*. Oxford: Oxford University Press.

Kress, G. (1991) Critical discourse analysis. *Annual Review of Applied Linguistics 1990*, 11, 84–99.

Kress, G. (1993) Genre as social process. In B. Kope and M. Kalantzis (eds) *The Powers of Literacy*. London: The Falmer Press.

Larsen-Freeman, D. (1991) An introduction to second language acquisition research: Staking out the territory. *TESOL Quarterly* 25, 315–50.

Larsen-Freeman, D. and Long, M. (1991) *An Introduction to Second Language Acquisition Research*. New York: Longman.

Lave, J. (1988) *Cognition in Practice: Mind, Mathematics and Culture in Everyday Life*. Cambridge: Cambridge University Press.

Lave, J. (1997) The culture of acquisition and the practice of understanding. In D. Kirshner and J.A. Whitson (eds) *Situated Cognition: Social, Semiotic and Psychological Perspectives*. Mahwah, NJ: Lawrence Erlbaum.

Lave, J. and Wenger, E. (1991) *Situated Learning: Legitimate Peripheral Participation*. Cambridge: Cambridge University Press.

Lee, E. (1985) *Letters to Marcia: A Teacher's Guide to Anti-racist Education*. Toronto: Cross Cultural Communication Centre.

Lemke, J. (1990) *Talking Science: Language, Learning and Values.* Norwood, NJ: Ablex.

Lensmire, T. (1996) *When Children Write: Critical Re-visions of the Writing Workshop.* New York: Teachers College Press.

Leontiev, A.N. (1981) The problem of activity in psychology. In J. Wertsch (ed.) *The Concept of Activity in Soviet Psychology.* Armonk, NY: Sharpe.

Leung, C., Harris, R. and Rampton, B. (1997) The idealised native speaker, reified ethnicities, and classroom realities. *TESOL Quarterly* 31, 543–60.

Levine, J. (ed.) (1990) *Bilingual Learners and the Mainstream Curriculum.* London: The Falmer Press.

Litowitz, B. (1997) Just say no: Responsibility and resistance. In M. Cole, Y. Engeström and O. Vasquez (eds) *Mind, Culture and Activity: Seminal Papers from the Laboratory of Human Cognition.* Cambridge: Cambridge University Press.

Lobel, A. (1982) *Ming Lo Moves the Mountain.* New York: Scholastic.

Long, M.H. (1977) Group work in the teaching and learning of English as a foreign language – problems and potential. *English Language Teaching Journal* 31, 285–92.

Long, M.H. (1981) Input, interaction and second language acquisition. In H. Winitz (ed.) *Native Language and Foreign Language Acquisition.* New York: New York Academy of Sciences, 379, 250–78.

Long, M.H., Adams, L., McLean, M. and Castanos, F. (1976) Doing things with words: Verbal interaction in lockstep and small group classroom situations. In R. Crymes and J. Fanselow (eds) *On TESOL '76.* Washington, DC: TESOL.

Long, M.H. and Porter, P. (1985) Group work, interlanguage talk and second language acquisition. *TESOL Quarterly* 19, 207–28.

Luke, A. (1995) Text and discourse in education: An introduction to critical discourse analysis. In M. Apple (ed.) *Review of Research in Education* 21. Itasca: F.E. Peacock.

Maclean, R. (1996) Quick! Hide! Constructing a playground identity in the early weeks of school. *Language and Education* 10, 171–86.

MacLure, M. and French, P. (1981) A comparison of talk at home and at school. In G. Wells (ed.) *Learning through Interaction: The Study of Language Development.* Cambridge: Cambridge University Press.

Matthews, M. (1996) Addressing issues of peer rejection in child-centered classrooms. *Early Childhood Education Journal* 24, 93–7.

McDermott, R. (1988) Inarticulateness. In D. Tannen (ed.) *Linguistics in Context: Connecting Observation and Understanding.* Norwood, NJ: Ablex.

McDermott, R. (1993) The acquisition of a child by a learning disability. In S. Chaiklin and J. Lave (eds) *Understanding Practice: Perspectives on Activity and Context.* Cambridge: Cambridge University Press.

McKay, S. and Wong, S-L C. (1996) Multiple discourses, multiple identities: Investment and agency in second language learning among Chinese adolescent immigrant students. *Harvard Educational Review* 66, 577–606.

McNamee, S. (1992) Reconstructing identity: The communal construction of crisis. In S. McNamee and K. Gergen (eds) *Therapy as Social Construction*. London: Sage.

Measures, E., Quell, C. and Wells, G. (1997) A sociocultural perspective on classroom discourse. In B. Davies and D. Corson (eds) *Oral Discourse and Education, Vol. 3, Encyclopedia of Language and Education*. Dordrecht: Klewer Academic.

Mehan, H. (1993) Beneath the skin and between the ears: A case study in the politics of representation. In S. Chaiklin and J. Lave (eds) *Understanding Practice: Perspectives on Activity and Context*. Cambridge: Cambridge University Press.

Mercer, N. (1992) Talk for teaching and learning. In K. Norman (ed.) *Thinking Voices: The Work of the National Oracy Project*. London: Hodder & Stoughton (for the National Curriculum Council).

Miller, P. and Goodnow, J. (1995) Cultural practices: Toward an integration of culture and development. In J. Goodnow, P. Miller and F. Kessel (eds) *Cultural Practices as Contexts for Development*. San Francisco, CA: Jossey-Bass.

Moje, E.B. (1998) Changing our minds, changing our bodies: Power as embedded in research relations. Paper presented at the American Educational Research Association meetings, San Diego, CA.

Moll, L.C. (1992) Bilingual classroom studies and community analysis: Some recent trends. *Educational Researcher* 21, 20–4.

Moll, L.C. (ed.) (1994) *Vygotsky and Education: Instructional Implications and Applications of Sociohistorical Psychology*. Cambridge: Cambridge University Press.

Morgan, B. (1997) Identity and intonation: Linking dynamic processes in an ESL classroom. *TESOL Quarterly* 31, 431–50.

Naiman, N., Fröhlich, M., Stern, H. and Todesco, A. (1978) *The Good Language Learner*. Toronto: OISE Press.

Newman, D., Griffin, P. and Cole, M. (1989). *The Construction Zone: Working for Cognitive Change in School*. Cambridge: Cambridge University Press.

Nietzsche, F. (1969) *On the Geneology of Morals*. New York: Vintage.

Norton Peirce, B. (1989) Toward a pedagogy of possibility in the teaching of English internationally: People's English in South Africa. *TESOL Quarterly* 23, 401–20.

Norton Peirce, B. (1995) Social identity, investment, and language learning. *TESOL Quarterly* 29, 9–31.

Norton, B. (ed.) (1997a) Language and identity. Special Issue *TESOL Quarterly* 31 (3).

Norton, B. (1997b) Language, identity, and the ownership of English. *TESOL Quarterly* 31 (3), 409–30.

Norton, B. (2000) *Identity and Language Learning:Gender, Ethnicity and Educational Change*. London: Longman.

Nunan, D. (1992) *Research Methods in Language Learning*. Cambridge: Cambridge University Press.

Nystrand, M., Gamoran, A., Kachur, R. and Prendergast, C. (1997) *Opening Dialogue: Understanding the Dynamics of Language Classrooms*. New York: Teachers College Press.

Ochs, E. (1988) *Culture and Language Development: Language Acquisition and Language Socialization in a Samoan Village*. Cambridge: Cambridge University Press.

Ochs, E. (1996) Linguistic resources for socializing humanity. In J. Gumperz and S. Levinson (eds) *Rethinking Linguistic Relativity*. Cambridge: Cambridge University Press.

Packer, M. (1993) Away from internalization. In E. Forman, N. Minick, and C. A. Stone (eds) *Contexts for Learning: Sociocultural Dynamics in Children's Development*. New York: Oxford University Press.

Paley, V.G. (1986) *Boys and Girls: Superheroes in the Doll Corner*. Chicago: University of Chicago Press.

Paley, V.G. (1989) *White Teacher*. Cambridge, MA: Harvard University Press.

Paley, V.G. (1992) *You Can't Say You Can't Play*. Cambridge, MA: Harvard University Press.

Paley, V.G. (1996) *Kwanzaa and Me: A Teacher's Story*. Cambridge, MA: Harvard University Press.

Patthey-Chavez, G., Clare, L. and Gallimore, R. (1995) *Creating a Community of Scholarship with Instructional Conversations in a Transitional Bilingual Classroom*. Washington, DC: Office of Educational Research and Improvement.

Pennycook, A. (1990) Toward a critical Applied Linguistics for the 1990s. *Issues in Applied Linguistics* 1, 8–28.

Pica, T. (1987) Second language acqusition, social interaction and the classroom. *Applied Linguistics* 8, 3–21.

Pica, T. and Doughty, C. (1986) Input and interaction in the communicative language classroom: A comparison of teacher-fronted and group activities. In S. Gass and C. Madden (eds) *Input and Second Language Acquisition*. Rowley, MA: Newbury House.

Rampton, B. (1995) *Crossing: Language and Ethnicity Among Adolescents*. London: Longman.

Ravem, R. (1968) Language acquisition in a second language environment. *International Review of Applied Linguistics* 6, 175–85.

Richards, J. (ed.) (1974) *Error Analysis*. New York: Longman.

Rigg, P. and Allen, V. (eds) (1989) *When They Don't All Speak English: Integrating the ESL Student into the Regular Classroom*. Urbana: NCTE.

Roberts, C. (1997) Transcribing talk: Issues of representation. *TESOL Quarterly* 31, 167–71.

Rogoff, B. (1990) *Apprenticeship in Thinking: Cognitive Development in Social Context*. New York: Oxford University Press.

Rogoff, B. (1994) Developing understanding of the idea of communities of learners. *Mind, Culture and Activity* 1, 209–29.

Rogoff, B., Mosier, C., Mistry, J., and Göncü, A. (1993) Toddler's guided participation with their caregivers in cultural activity. In E. Forman, N. Minick and C.A. Stone (eds) *Contexts for Learning: Sociocultural Dynamics in Children's Development*. New York: Oxford University Press.

Rogoff, B., Matusov, E., and White, C. (1996) Models of teaching and learning: Participation in a community of learners. In D. Olson and N. Torrance (eds) *The Handbook of Education and Human Development: New Models of Learning, Teaching and Schooling*. Oxford: Blackwell.

Romaine, S. (1995) *Bilingualism (Language in Society, No. 13)* (2nd edn). Oxford: Blackwell.

Rosa, A. and Montero, I. (1994) The historical context of Vygotsky's work: A sociohistorical approach. In L.C. Moll (ed.) *Vygotsky and Education: Instructional Implications and Applications of Sociohistorical Psychology*. Cambridge: Cambridge University Press.

Rubin, J. (1975) What the 'good language learner' can tell us. *TESOL Quarterly* 9, 41–51.

Ryan, W. (1989) Disciplining the Innut: Normalization, characterization, and schooling. *Curriculum Inquiry* 19, 379–404.

Sampson, E.D. (1989) The challenge of social change for psychology: Globalization and psychology's theory of the person. *American Psychologist* 44, 914–21.

Saville-Troike, M. (1988) Private speech: Evidence for second language strategies during the 'silent' period. *Journal of Child Language* 15, 567–90.

Schachter, J. (1988) Second language acquisition and its relationship to Universal Grammar. *Applied Linguistics*, 9, 219–35.

Schachter, J. and Celce-Murcia, M. (1977) Some reservations concerning error analysis. *TESOL Quarterly* 11, 441–51.

Selinker, L. (1972) Interlanguage. *International Review of Applied Linguistics* 10, 210–31.

Shuy, R. (1981) Learning to talk like teachers. *Language Arts* 58, 168–74.

Smolka, A.L., De Goes, M.C. and Pins, A. (1995) The constitution of the subject: A persistent question. In J. Wertsch, P. Del Ris and A. Alvarez (eds) *Sociocultural Studies of Mind*. Cambridge: Cambridge University Press.

Snow, C.E. (1987) Beyond conversation: Second language learners' acquisition of description and explanation. In J. Lantolf and A. Labarca (eds) *Research in Second Language Learning: Focus on the Classroom*. Norwood, NJ: Ablex.

Snow, C.E. (1992) Perspectives on second-language development: Implications for bilingual education. *Educational Researcher*, 16–19.

Snow, C.E. (1993) Bilingualism and second language acquisition. In J. Berko Gleason and N. Bernstein Ratner (eds) *Psycholinguistics*. Fort Worth, TX: Harcourt Brace Jovanovich College.

Snow, C.E. and Hoefnagel-Höhle, M. (1978) The critical period for language acquisition: Evidence from second language learning. *Child Development* 49, 1114–28.

Strong, M. (1983) Social styles and the second language acquisition of Spanish-speaking kindergarteners. *TESOL Quarterly* 17, 241–59.

Swain, M. and Lapkin, S. (1982) *Evaluating Bilingual Education: A Canadian Case Study*. Clevedon, Avon: Multilingual Matters.

Taylor, C. (1989) *Sources of the Self: The Making of the Modern Identity*. Cambridge, MA: Harvard University Press.

Taylor, C. (1994) *Multiculturalism: Examining the Politics of Recognition*. Princeton, NJ: Princeton University Press.

Tharp, R. and Gallimore, R. (1991) *The Instructional Conversation: Teaching and Learning in Social Activity*. Washington, DC: Office of Educational Research and Improvement.

Toohey, K. (1996) Learning English as a second language in kindergarten: A community of practice perspective. *The Canadian Modern Language Review* 52, 549–76.

Toohey, K. (1998) 'Breaking them up; taking them away': ESL students in grade one. *TESOL Quarterly* 32, 61–84.

Toohey, K., Waterstone, B. and Julé-Lemke, A. (2000). Community of learners, carnival and participation in a Punjabi Sikh classroom. *The Canadian Modern Language Review* 56, 423–438.

Tootoosis, V. (1983) Oral language and learning of one five year old Cree child at home and at school. Unpublished Masters thesis, University of Alberta, Edmonton.

Trueba, H., Guthrie, G.P. and Au, K. (eds) (1981) *Culture and the Bilingual Classroom: Studies in Classroom Ethnography*. Rowley, MA: Newbury House.

Varga, D. (1998) The dynamics of children's alienated play. *Canadian Journal of Research in Early Childhood Education* 6, 313–25.

Vasquez, O.A., Pease-Alvarez, L. and Shannon, S.M. (1994) *Pushing Boundaries: Language and Culture in a Mexican Community*. New York: Cambridge University Press.

Vygotsky, L.S. (1978) *Mind in Society: The Development of Higher Psychological Processes*. Cambridge, MA: Harvard University Press.

Vygotsky, L.S. (1981) The instrumental method in psychology. In J. Wertsch (ed.) *The Concept of Activity in Soviet Psychology*. Armonk, NY: Sharpe.

Vygotsky, L.S. (1986) *Thought and Language* (trans. A. Kozulin). Cambridge, MA: The MIT Press.

Walkerdine, V. (1988) *The Mastery of Reason*. London: Routledge.

Walkerdine, V. (1997) Redefining the subject in situated cognition theory. In D. Kirshner and J.A. Whitson (eds) *Situated Cognition: Social, Semiotic and Psychological Perspectives*. Mahwah, NJ: Lawrence Erlbaum.

Waller, W. (1961) *The Sociology of Teaching*. New York: Russell & Russell.

Wells, G. (1986) *The Meaning Makers: Children Learning Language and Using Language to Learn.* Portsmouth, NH: Heinemann Educational Books, Inc.

Wells, G. (1993) Reevaluating the IRF sequence: A proposal for the articulation of theories of activity and discourse for the analysis of teaching and learning in the classroom. *Linguistics and Education* 5, 1–37.

Wells, G. and Chang-Wells, G.L. (1992) *Constructing Knowledge Together: Classrooms as Centers of Inquiry and Literacy.* Portsmouth, NH: Heinemann.

Wertsch, J. (1991) *Voices of the Mind: A Sociocultural Approach to Mediated Action.* Cambridge, MA: Harvard University Press.

Wertsch, J. (1998) *Mind as Action.* New York: Oxford University Press.

Wertsch, J., del Río, P. and Alvarez, A. (eds) (1995) *Sociocultural Studies of Mind.* New York: Oxford University Press.

White, P. (1998) RE: Confused in California. Contribution to xmca list. Available: http://communication.ucsd.edu/MCA/Mail/xmcamail.9801.dir/0123.html

Willett, J. (1995) Becoming first graders in an L2: An ethnographic study of language socialization. *TESOL Quarterly* 29, 473–504.

Wong Fillmore, L. (1979) Individual differences in second language acquisition. In C. Fillmore, D. Kempler and W. Wang (eds) *Individual Differences in Language Ability and Language Behavior.* New York: Academic Press.

Wood, D. (1992) Teaching talk. In K. Norman (ed.) *Thinking Voices: The Work of the National Oracy Project.* London: Hodder & Stoughton (for the National Curriculum Council).

Wood, D., Bruner, J.S. and Ross, G. (1976) The role of tutoring in problem-solving. *Journal of Child Psychology and Psychiatry*, 89–100.

Woolf, V. (1977) *Books and Portraits: Some Further Selections from the Literary and Biographical Writings of Virginia Woolf.* New York: Harcourt Brace Jovanovitch College.

Index

Author Index

Agre, P., 77
Allen, V., 1
Appel, G., 2, 9
Applebaum, S. D., 9, 93
Baker, C. D., 122
Bakhtin, M., 12, 13, 16, 60, 99, 100, 121, 124, 126, 128, 133
Bell, J., 132-33
Berk, L., 74
Berron, C., 59
Birdwhistell, R., 106
Bochner, S., 93
Bordo, S., 130, 132
Bourdieu, P., 2, 111
Bourne, J., 9
Brislin, R. W., 93
Bryson, M., 8, 68
Burt, M., 1,7
Cazden, C., 10, 94, 98, 99, 100, 117
Celce-Murcia, M., 7
Chang-Wells, G. L., 2, 10
Clandinin, J., 132
Cole, M., 2, 9
Collins, J., 15
Connelly, M., 132
Corder, P., 7
Corsaro, D., 111
Dagenais, D., 59
Davis, K., 7, 9, 16
Day, E., 134
de Castell, S., 8, 68
Doughty, C., 105
Duff, P., 72
Dulay, H., 1,7
Duranti, A., 9
Edwards, A. D., 100, 116, 117

Eisenhart, M., 78, 118
Ellis, R., 1, 7
Ervin-Tripp, S., 60
Evans, K.S., 133
Faltis, C., 1
Fine, M., 66
Forman, E., 15, 134
Foucault, M., 2, 8, 61, 62, 77, 90, 126, 132
Freire, P., 94
French, P., 100
Furnham, A., 93
Gal, S., 8, 126
Gallimore, R., 128
Genesee, F., 1
Gibbons, P., 1
Goffman, E., 72
Goodman, K., 10
Goodman, Y., 10
Goodnow, J., 81
Goodwin, C., 9
Goodwin, M. H., 9, 70, 111
Goldenberg, C., 128
Grumet, M., 124
Gumperz, J., 2
Gutierrez, K., 9, 100, 115, 116, 117, 122, 129
Hakuta, K., 7, 60
Hall, J. K., 2, 60, 75, 81, 99, 100, 115, 117, 122, 128
Hall, S., 8, 126, 129
Hanks, W., 14
Hatch, E., 7, 60
Hazzard, S., 80
Hicks, D., 135
Hoefnagel-Höhle, M., 1
Holland, D., 118
Huang, J., 7

Subject Index